MY HEALING JOURNEY GUIDED BY MODERN SCIENCE AND ANCIENT WISDOM

By Anjali Walia DeSure

TABLE OF CONTENTS

Chapter 1: Karma From Past Lives
Chapter 2: Sohan Lal, the Reserved One
Chapter 3: Susheila, the Song Bird
Chapter 4: Gaura Devi, My Look-Alike
Chapter 5: Hanuman the Divine Helper
Chapter 6: Saraswati Devi, Goddess of Learning
Chapter 7: Jagdish, the Durga Devotee
Chapter 8: Offering to Durga
Chapter 9: Father's Departure
Chapter 10: Sukshma Sharira, Home of the Chakras
Chapter 11: Ganesha, Lord of the Five Sense Organs
Chapter 12: Shiva, the First Yogi
Chapter 13: Krishna, the Diplomat
Chapter 14: SwarBhanu, the Clever Dragon
Chapter 15: Brihaspati, Teacher of the Gods
Chapter 16: Complex Post Traumatic Stress Disorder
Chapter 17: Order in Chaos
Chapter 18: Arrival of Lakshmi
Chapter 19: Panchanguli Devi, Goddess of Five Fingers
Chapter 20: The Human Form, a Tool for Tantra
Chapter 21: Ma Kali, The Transformer

COPYRIGHT PAGE

Copyright © 2024 by Anjali Walia DeSure

All rights reserved. No part of this publication may be reproduced, distributed, or transmitted in any form or by any means, including photocopying, recording, or other electronic or mechanical methods, without the prior written permission of the author, except in the case of brief quotations embodied in critical reviews and certain other noncommercial uses permitted by copyright law.

This memoir reflects the author's recollections of experiences over time. Some names and identifying details have been changed to protect the privacy of individuals.

First Edition

ISBN: 979-8-9992084-1-5

AUTHOR'S NOTE

This memoir chronicles a journey from childhood trauma to spiritual awakening, weaving together personal narrative with teachings from Vedic wisdom traditions. The experiences described reflect my own healing process and should not be considered medical or psychological advice. Readers dealing with trauma are encouraged to seek professional support from qualified practitioners.

The Sanskrit terms and spiritual concepts presented here represent my understanding gained through study and practice. I acknowledge that these ancient teachings contain depths of wisdom that far exceed any individual interpretation.

PREFACE

In a world increasingly divided between the rational and the mystical, Anjali Walia DeSure offers us something extraordinary: a roadmap for healing that honors both the precision of modern trauma research and the profound wisdom of ancient Vedic traditions.

This memoir is not merely a personal story—it is a bridge. A bridge between East and West, between the analytical mind and the intuitive heart, between the cellular memory of trauma and the cellular possibility of transformation.

This book weaves together insights from neuroscience, Ayurveda, astrology, somatic therapy, and personal revelation into a tapestry that honors the full spectrum of human experience. Dr. Bessel van der Kolk's groundbreaking work on how "the body keeps the score" finds its complement in the ancient understanding of chakras as centers of stored experience. Peter Levine's somatic experiencing resonates with yogic practices that have guided seekers for millennia.

The author's journey from a traumatized child in 1960s Delhi to a woman capable of deep self-compassion and healing offers hope to anyone who has ever wondered if transformation is truly possible. Her story illustrates that healing happens not despite our wounds, but through our willingness to meet them with consciousness, courage, and the right combination of ancient wisdom and modern understanding.

Perhaps most importantly, this memoir demonstrates that the precious human form—what Buddhist teachers call as rare as "a blind turtle surfacing through a ring in the vast ocean"—is indeed the perfect vehicle for awakening. Through her exploration of everything from Vedic astrology to plant medicine, from palmistry to nervous system regulation, Anjali shows us that every aspect of our being—physical, emotional, mental, and spiritual—can become a doorway to freedom.

This is a book for anyone who has ever felt broken and wondered if wholeness was possible. It is for trauma survivors seeking integration, for spiritual seekers wanting to ground their practice in embodied reality, and for anyone curious about how ancient wisdom traditions can inform modern healing.

As you read these pages, you are invited not just to witness one woman's healing journey, but to consider your own. For in the end, this memoir is not just Anjali's story—it is a mirror reflecting the universal human capacity for transformation, growth, and the endless possibility of beginning again.

May all beings find their way to healing.
May all beings discover the wisdom hidden within their wounds.
May all beings awaken to their true nature.

CHAPTER 1
Karma From Past Lives

Two and a half months before my twenty-eighth birthday, on a balmy March afternoon in California, I found myself standing at the threshold of a truth I wasn't ready to hear. The Southern California sunshine filtered through scattered clouds like light through temple screens, creating patterns of shadow and illumination that seemed to mirror the uncertainty churning within my soul. The air carried that peculiar stillness—the calm before a storm that would reshape everything, I thought I knew about my life.

I had been in America for seven years now, long enough to shed many of my Indian sensibilities but not quite long enough to feel fully American.

The quiet residential street in Santa Monica was lined with low-rise concrete and wood multi-family dwellings. Next to the street parking, a massive jacaranda tree bloomed with purple blossoms. The tree beckoned tiny yellow finches whose melodious chirping struck something deep within me as I approached the wooden staircase leading to the second floor.

One hundred and five pounds of doubt and hope, hung on a five ft 3-inch frame climbed those creaky wooden steps, my body tingling with the mixture of anticipation and dread. The Vedic astrologer—or *Jyotishi* as we call them in India—I was about to consult lived an ocean away from his traditional peers yet only a ten-minute drive from the Santa Monica townhouse where Ken had recently committed to a one-year lease. That townhouse represented more than just a change of address; it was Ken's way of saying he was ready for us to build something permanent together. He had also surprised me with a sizable diamond solitaire.

The engagement ring felt foreign on my finger—beautiful but heavy with implications. I had removed it twice since Ken proposed, not out of rejection but out of the overwhelming sense that accepting it meant crossing a bridge I couldn't uncross. In my culture, marriage was not just the union of two individuals but the merging of families, destinies, karmas. I had already failed at this sacred institution twice. Did I dare risk my heart—and Ken's—on a third attempt?

My inner voice, that persistent companion, chimed with her familiar mix of wisdom and worry: *Anjali, you've never been loved like this before. But are you ready to make a lifetime commitment?* She paused, *no, I don't think so.*

The honesty of my inner voice often startled me. She was the part of me that remembered the little girl who had learned early that love could be dangerous, that commitment could become a cage, that even the people who were supposed to protect you could fail in devastating ways.

My teeth found their familiar target on my lower lip—a nervous habit I had carried since childhood. "But the divorce with Mahesh is finally over," I replied to myself, speaking silently to that inner witness who knew all my secrets. "I want to have a child. Ken will make a good father."

My inner voice reprimanded with the stern love: *Anjali, live by yourself for a while. First, you have to befriend your fears. You've already changed your last name three times.*

Three times. Born Anjali Ahluwalia, I had become Anjali Malik through my first marriage, then reverted to Anjali Walia after the divorce, then Anjali Goklaney through my second marriage, then reverted back to Anjali Walia and now faced the prospect of becoming Anjali Desure if I said yes to Ken's proposal.

"Please, Kenneth, can't we just live together for now and see how it works out?" I had pleaded the night he proposed, my voice small with vulnerability.

Ken had pulled me closer, his arms creating the kind of safety I had rarely experienced. His response carried both patience and gentle humor: "Of course. I'll wait until this box of Q-tips is empty, and then I'll propose again."

Kenneth was the exact opposite of Mahesh. Mahesh practiced psychiatry but was a frustrated artist at heart. He approached life with the intensity of someone who felt the world owed him more recognition than it had provided. Kenneth made a good living as a chiropractor but was a Tantric Buddhist at soul level, approaching both his work and his spirituality with steady dedication.

Ken was a breath of fresh air while Mahesh had gone stale in the span of just one year—though I understood now that the staleness had probably been there from the beginning, masked by the excitement of new love and shared cultural understanding. Ken carried Polish and Ukrainian Jewish ancestral wisdom in his bones, stories of survival and adaptation. Mahesh was the typical product of middle-class Indian parents aspiring for more in the material world—brilliant, ambitious, but somehow disconnected from the deeper currents of meaning that made life worth living.

For this meeting with the Vedic astrologer, I had chosen my clothes with the unconscious care of someone preparing for a ritual. The loose-fitting white cotton blouse and pants felt both comfortable and appropriate—white being the color of openness to whatever truth might emerge. The long purple scarf adorned with paisley motifs that I draped around my neck carried the colors of transformation and the ancient patterns that connected me to the unbroken chain of Indian women who had consulted astrologers about their destinies for thousands of years.

The front door to the apartment stood slightly ajar, as if the astrologer had sensed my approach. He waited behind it, a dark silhouette against the dimly lit interior. He gestured with his hands to invite me in.

"*Namaskar*, Pandit-ji. I am Anjali." I pressed both palms together in front of my heart, feeling the familiar comfort of this greeting that acknowledged the divine spark in both the giver and receiver.

His clean-shaven head nodded in response. His dark skin seemed to radiate the moist heat of Southern India. Between his thinning eyebrows sat a smear of sandalwood paste—the traditional *tilak* that marked him as a serious practitioner. I guessed that he was in his mid-sixties. Thick glasses softened his intense dark pupils but couldn't completely mask the penetrating quality of his gaze.

After depositing my sandals next to the closed front door—a small act that transported me instantly back to every temple and traditional home I had ever entered—I looked up and gasped. At the end of the dimly lit room, under a five-foot-tall wooden pergola, stood a four-foot bronze statue of Shiva, glowing as he performed his eternal dance of creation and destruction.

The sight of Nataraja—Shiva as the Lord of Dance—in this modest Santa Monica apartment created a portal between worlds. Here was the cosmic principle of transformation made manifest in bronze, every detail of the statue conveying layers of meaning.

Shiva's third eye blazed wide open with the fire of divine perception, while his other two eyes remained closed in the deepest meditation. This was the paradox of ultimate consciousness—simultaneously engaged with the world of form and completely transcendent of it. Strands of matted hair caressed his shoulders, swirling in rhythm with his head moving from side to side in the eternal dance of creation and destruction.

His four arms—signifying the four cardinal directions—were fully engaged in the cosmic choreography. He balanced perfectly on his right foot, while his left leg was held up at a forty-five-degree angle.

Shiva's upper right hand held a *damaru*, the small hourglass drum whose rhythm creates the fundamental vibrations from which all of creation emerges. This was the cosmic heartbeat. His lower right hand formed the *abhaya mudra*—the gesture of "freedom from fear"—with forearm perpendicular to his body and wrist held parallel to the ground. Four fingers stood straight while his thumb bent at the first knuckle toward his palm.

Shiva's upper left hand held a flaming torch, the eternal fire that drives darkness away and represents the light of consciousness. His lower left hand pointed gracefully down toward his right foot, beneath which lay trapped Apasmara, the "dwarf of ignorance"—that aspect of consciousness that forgets its divine nature and becomes lost in the maze of ego and identification.

On the floor below this magnificent statue, a cheap plastic tray held the essential items for *puja*—the worship ritual that connects the devotee with the divine presence. The astrologer had offered Shiva a clay lamp filled with oil, its small flame flickering like a captured star. An incense stick planted in a ceramic bowl of rice kernels spread the smoke and scent of sandalwood throughout the room. A ripe banana and a bright tangerine completed the offering—simple fruits that represented the sweetness of surrender and the abundance that flows from aligning with cosmic principles.

The astrologer sat cross-legged on a worn brown rug facing Shiva, dressed entirely in white cotton. An ancient book wrapped in red silk rested in his lap, immediately drawing my attention with its promise of hidden knowledge.

He pointed toward a shriveled gray bean bag positioned to his left side—my designated seat in this cosmic consultation. Above it, on the wall, hung a two-foot-square glass-framed picture of Parvati that seemed to glow with its own inner light.

Shiva's eternal consort—Shakti, incarnated as Parvati—was

depicted in her aspect as the supreme yogini, meditating beneath the sprawling green canopy of a mature banyan tree. Her milky white skin contrasted beautifully with her long blue-black hair. Above her closed eyes, perfectly centered between elegantly arched eyebrows, rested a red *bindu*—the sacred dot that marked her as an awakened being.

Her sensuous curves were draped in a pristine white sari that seemed to be woven from moonbeams, while her graceful neck was adorned with a string of *rudraksha* beads representing the "tears of Shiva."

She sat with legs crossed in the perfect lotus pose, her right foot resting on her left thigh and vice versa, demonstrating the mastery over physical limitations that comes with deep spiritual practice. Her forearms rested on her thighs with the relaxed alertness of one who has found perfect equilibrium between effort and surrender. Both hands formed the *chin mudra*—the gesture of "communion with the divine"—with middle finger and thumb touching to create a closed circuit of energy, ring finger bent at its top and middle joints, while pointer and pinky fingers stood straight like antennas receiving cosmic transmission.

Above Parvati's left shoulder, in the banyan's dense thicket, a magnificent peacock perched on a branch alongside birds of various feathers—parrots, mynas, and kingfishers—while squirrels and langur monkeys rested among other branches.

Gathered around Parvati at the base of the tree, their eyes filled with bliss, were lions, cows, ducks, elephants, deer, and wolves. Natural enemies sat in perfect harmony; their predatory instincts dissolved in the presence of one who had transcended the dualities that create conflict. This was the vision of *ahimsa*—non-violence—that emerges when consciousness recognizes its own unity in all forms.

The story of Shiva and Parvati represented the most profound love affair in Hindu mythology—not the romantic love of popular imagination, but the cosmic romance between consciousness and its own creative power. Shakti, in her incarnation as Parvati, had undergone the most severe penance —*tapasya*—to win Shiva's attention and love. She had taken multiple births as Lakshmi (abundance), Kamala (lotus-born wisdom), Saraswati (knowledge), Durga (protective fierceness), Kali (transformative destruction), and countless other forms, while Shiva remained forever the unchanging witness—never born, never dying, always present.

The Vedas state that Brahman—the Atma, the individual soul —is part of cosmic consciousness, the fundamental singularity that gives rise to the apparent duality of Shiva and Shakti. According to traditional understanding, Shiva consciousness resides in the right half of the human body, connected to the logical, analytical functions of the left brain. Shakti energy lives on the left side of the body, under the influence of the right brain's holistic, intuitive intelligence.

Modern neuroscience had begun to validate these ancient insights. British psychiatrist, neuroscientist, and philosopher Dr. Iain McGilchrist, author of *The Master and His Emissary*, had mapped different value systems to each brain hemisphere: the left hemisphere focuses on rules, measurements, and categorical thinking, while the right hemisphere inclines toward the holistic, mystical, and interconnected understanding of reality.

As I settled uncomfortably on the bean bag, my inner voice offered her characteristic mix of encouragement and brutal honesty: *Sparks of Shakti Spring from you now and then, Anjali. Even though your skin is nowhere near the porcelain white that Indian beauty standards prefer, people still find you attractive. But do you find yourself lovable?*

A minute of my twists and turns on the soft bean bag gave the pandit adequate time to study my astrological chart and form his firm opinion. The red silk book lay open in his lap; its yellowed pages covered with Sanskrit calculations and diagrams that traced the cosmic influences.

Focused intently on a particular page, he cleared his throat. When he spoke, his words fell like stones into still water, creating ripples that would disturb my peace for years to come: "According to this chart, your father failed. He failed in his dharma toward you."

The words hit me like a physical blow. I squealed in protest, my voice rising to a pitch that embarrassed me even as I couldn't control it: "No! Pandit-ji, are you sure? I don't know my exact time of birth."

My inner voice whispered with protective fury: *He's a pompous pig who doesn't know anything about your father's love.*

But the astrologer continued with the relentless certainty of one reading from a cosmic script. His eyes remained glued to the ominous red book as he replied, "Madam, this *is* the correct chart. Based on the information *you* provided, I have calculated the proper birth time using rectification techniques."

My head lowered as my eyes found refuge in examining my sweaty palms, those traitorous appendages that always revealed my emotional state no matter how much I tried to project calm. The lines etched across my palms seemed to tell their own story —lifeline, heart line, fate line all intersecting in patterns that perhaps confirmed what this stranger was telling me about my childhood.

My inner voice wailed: *Hai Ram, Anjali! You may be unaware of your exact birth time, but you're certainly aware of how much your father loved and cared for you.*

But the astrologer continued his relentless litany, eyes still fixed on the red book as he delivered more ominous pronouncements in the same monotone voice he might use to read a grocery list. My ears began to ache. I tried to focus instead on the rhythmic whirring of the old ceiling fan, its steady rotation a meditative counterpoint to the chaos being unleashed in my mind.

Minutes flew by in a haze of discomfort and denial before my obvious lack of attention became evident to him. "Do you have any more questions?" he asked, and I detected no trace of sympathy in his voice, no acknowledgment that he had just delivered news that shattered a daughter's most precious memories.

I looked up, my eyes coming to rest on Parvati's serene image. Her face radiated the peace of one who had endured the most severe trials and emerged with love intact. My inner voice sighed: *Anjali, if you pay him even a single penny, you will tear your father's memory limb from limb.*

"Pandit-ji, I left my checkbook in the car. I'll be right back." The words flew from my mouth as I straightened my back and stood with the sudden urgency of someone fleeing a burning building.

The lie felt justified. I needed to escape before his predictions could embed themselves any deeper in my psyche.

The pandit scratched his nose with the resignation of one accustomed to clients who couldn't handle the truth he dispensed. His eyes narrowed slightly as his head nodded in acknowledgment, though we both knew I wasn't coming back.

With pursed lips and clenched fists, I rushed down the creaky wooden stairs. My body crashed like a sack of potatoes onto the driver's seat of my golden Toyota Cressida, and suddenly the familiar confines of my car felt like the most sacred space in the world.

My inner voice, now free to express her full indignation, wailed: *This man has no heart! No mention of any good fortune coming your way, no acknowledgment of your strengths or gifts. What did your father do to you that was so terrible? But you always knew deep down, didn't you—something is fundamentally wrong with you.*

This was the fear I carried in my deepest places—that there was something wrong with me. The astrologer's words had activated this ancient wound with surgical precision.

As I straightened in the car seat, my inner voice offered the kindest counsel she could manage: *Anjali, stay in the car. Have a good cry. Let it all out before you drive home to Ken's questions about how the reading went.*

But I shook my head, knowing that remaining in this place would only deepen the wounds that had been opened. I turned the key in my almost new Toyota Cressida, grateful for its safety features that were far superior to the two old cars I had totaled since arriving in the USA seven years ago. Those accidents had been learning experiences about American roads and American driving habits, but they had also served as metaphors for my entire immigrant experience—a series of crashes and recoveries as I navigated unfamiliar terrain.

A year later, when repressed memories from my childhood surfaced during therapy like debris rising from the depths of a disturbed lake, I would realize with shocking clarity how wrong I had been to question the pandit's assessment of my father failing me.

The astrologer's pronouncement about my father's failure hadn't been cruelty or pompousness—it had been frank truth-telling from someone trained to read the cosmic signatures of our deepest wounds. He had seen in the planetary positions my dridha karma (fixed karma) at the time and location of my birth. I had incarnated to transform my consciousness. But he failed to talk about the adridha karma, the karma which can be changed by willpower and discipline. This karma definitely shows up in the lines and signs on the two palms.

As I merged into the familiar flow of Los Angeles traffic, the physical act of driving became a meditation. The astrologer had cracked open the shell of my carefully constructed identity, and I wasn't yet ready for what might emerge from the darkness.

The ring on my finger caught the afternoon light as I gripped the steering wheel, its sparkle a reminder of Ken's love waiting for me at home.

The astrologer's words would echo in my mind for months and years to come, growing in significance.

CHAPTER 2
Sohan Lal, the Reserved One

In the sweltering summer of 1947, as the monsoon clouds gathered over the Indian subcontinent, the British Empire made its final decision about the jewel in its crown. After three centuries of colonial rule, they were finally departing—but not before leaving behind a legacy that would scar the land and its people for generations.

As the British administrators scurried out of the Indian subcontinent, they left behind the hastily carved remnants of their former colony: the new nation of India, where Hindus formed a majority, and Pakistan—split impossibly into two wings separated by a thousand miles of Indian territory—where Muslims would find their promised homeland.

What followed was one of the largest forced migrations in human history, a human tsunami that swept across the newly created borders. One million people were massacred in the name of religion. Fifteen million more became refugees overnight, carrying nothing but the clothes on their backs and memories of homes they would never see again.

Countless others, faced with the choice between flight and an uncertain fate at the hands of those who had become strangers overnight, chose a third option: they committed suicide, hoping for a better afterlife. It became tragically common for husbands and fathers to push their daughters and wives into deep wells, thereby sparing them from the indignities and violence at the hands of men driven mad by religious fervor and the intoxication of sudden, lawless power.

Against this backdrop of civilizational collapse, my father, Sohan Lal, was living what should have been the golden years of his young manhood. At twenty-three, he possessed the kind of quiet magnetism that drew people to him without effort. He was considered handsome by the standards of his time and community, despite his skin being several shades darker than the wheat-colored complexion that Punjabi society deemed most attractive.

The twinkle in Papa's warm brown eyes was sustained by an unquenchable thirst for knowledge, a curiosity about the world that made conversations with him feel like explorations of uncharted territories.

His parents' failure to arrange a suitable marriage for their dutiful eldest son had nothing to do with any lack in his marriageability—he was educated, employed, handsome, and possessed of the kind of gentle temperament that made him a favorite among both his students and colleagues. Rather, the family was still reeling from a tragedy that had shaken them to their core: the sudden loss of a bright and healthy teenage son to smallpox just a year and half prior.

Sohan Lal held a coveted teaching position at the prestigious Lahore College, the same institution where he had earned his master's degree with a double major in mathematics and psychology—an unusual combination that reflected his belief that understanding the human mind required both logical precision and intuitive insight. He taught mathematics to engineering students.

His daily practice of Hatha yoga had blessed him with a muscular, broad chest. But it was his mind, not his body, that truly set him apart. He approached yoga not as mere physical exercise but as a complete system for integrating body, mind, and spirit.

He was a regular at the Vedanta Society, a branch of the Ramakrishna Mission that had been established by the legendary Swami Vivekananda. Vivekananda had been the first teacher to bring Vedic wisdom to the West, addressing the World Parliament of Religions in Chicago in 1893 with such eloquence and insight that he had opened Western minds to the possibility that profound spiritual wisdom might come from the East rather than flowing only from West to East. As a disciple of the great mystic Shri Ramakrishna Paramahansa, Vivekananda had understood that all religions were different paths to the same summit.

Sohan Lal's father, Kundan Lal, held the respected position of principal at the only high school in the town of Pindi Bhattian, a modest settlement on the outskirts of the great city of Lahore in the prosperous province of Punjab. The family name, Ahluwalia, connected them to a proud lineage of Sikh warriors and administrators, though they had converted to Hinduism generations earlier. This religious fluidity, common in Punjab where spiritual traditions had always cross-pollinated, would soon become a matter of life and death.

In the early spring of 1947, before the communal tensions that had been simmering beneath the surface of Indian society erupted into open warfare, Sohan Lal's sixteen-year-old brother, Rattan Lal, came to visit him in Lahore. The city was still the vibrant cultural capital it had been for centuries—a place where Hindu, Muslim, and Sikh artists, merchants, and intellectuals had created one of the subcontinent's most sophisticated urban cultures.

The two brothers, separated by seven years but united by deep affection and mutual respect, spent their time together as young men had for generations in that ancient city. They visited the magnificent Badshahi Mosque, its red sandstone walls and marble domes a testament to the Mughal architectural genius. They strolled through the narrow lanes of the old city, where the aroma of kulfi and samosas mixed with the incense from dozens of temples and the calls to prayer that echoed from mosques.

They witnessed the early signs of the exodus—Hindu families

loading their possessions onto bullock carts, speaking in hushed tones about properties they were trying to sell quickly. But like many optimistic young people, they believed that sanity would prevail, that the politicians and religious leaders would find a way to prevent the catastrophe that everyone could sense approaching.

The brothers stayed put, thinking that the great cosmopolitan city of Lahore, with its centuries of multicultural harmony, would surely end up in India when the final borders were drawn. How could the British possibly award this jewel of Punjabi culture to Pakistan? It seemed unthinkable that a city where Hindu, Muslim, and Sikh festivals were celebrated by people of all faiths could be carved away from the land where those traditions had been born.

The illusion of safety shattered overnight when a train from Delhi arrived in Lahore loaded with the dead and dying. The railway carriages had been transformed into mobile morgues. Bodies were stacked like cordwood, many showing signs of torture and mutilation that spoke to the depths of hatred that had been unleashed.

The bloodshed of Hindus in Lahore started that very night. Mobs armed with swords, axes, and an implacable conviction that they were doing God's work began moving through neighborhoods that had been home to Hindu families for generations. The sounds that filled the air—screams, the crash of breaking glass, the crackle of fires—created a symphony of civilization's collapse.

With no knowledge of their family's welfare or whereabouts, the two brothers made the desperate decision to attempt escape from a city that had become a death trap. The transportation options were limited and dangerous. Trains were being stopped and searched, cars were being pulled over at improvised checkpoints, and anyone attempting to leave on foot faced the certainty of encountering roving gangs of killers.

They managed to locate a truck that was leaving Lahore, packed beyond any reasonable safety limit with Hindu refugees who understood that overcrowding was preferable to staying behind. The truck driver, himself a refugee who was risking his life to save others, could only take one more passenger. The vehicle was already groaning under the weight of human cargo, and adding two persons might cause mechanical failure or, worse...

In a moment that would haunt him for the rest of his life, Sohan Lal made the choice that would define him as both a brother and a man. Without hesitation, he helped Rattan Lal climb onto the back of the truck and wished him a safe journey. As the eldest son, he believed his duty was to ensure his younger brother's survival, even if it meant sacrificing his own chances of escape.

The truck disappeared into the smoke and chaos of a city burning itself to death, carrying Rattan Lal toward an uncertain but hopeful future. Sohan Lal was left standing alone in the street, surrounded by the sounds of approaching violence, facing the prospect of death with the strange peace that comes to those who have chosen love over self-preservation.

When Rattan Lal finally reached the family's ancestral home in Patiala—a city in Punjab that had been allocated to India—he found that his parents, Gaura Devi and Kundan Lal, and his young sister and brother were already there. They had managed to escape from Pindi Bhattian with some of their possessions and most of their lives intact, but they carried with them the terrible uncertainty about the fate of their eldest son.

For months, they waited for news that never came. Had Sohan Lal survived the initial bloodshed? Had he been among the thousands who were killed in the first wave of violence? Was he hiding somewhere in the ruins of Lahore? Or had he joined the growing number of refugees making the dangerous journey on foot across the new border?

Gaura Devi, who had given birth to Sohan Lal when she was barely more than a child herself, found herself aging years in a matter of weeks. Kundan Lal, the respected educator who had always believed that knowledge and reason would triumph over ignorance and hatred, struggled to maintain his faith in human nature while fearing the worst about his beloved eldest son.

What they didn't know was that Sohan Lal, in the aftermath of his brother's departure, had found his way to a group of monks from the Vedanta Society who were preparing to undertake one of the most dangerous journeys imaginable: to travel on foot from Lahore to India's capital of Delhi.

The decision to join them was both practical and spiritual. Traveling alone as a young Hindu man would have been suicide, but a group of saffron-robed monks might be able to move through the countryside with less likelihood of being targeted.

He donned the saffron robes that marked him as a renunciant, hung a *rudraksha* bead mala around his neck like a rosary of protection, and tucked a begging bowl under his arm. In this disguise, he began what would become a nine-week odyssey across a landscape transformed into a battlefield.

The journey from Lahore to Delhi would normally take a few days by train or a week by bullock cart. On foot, avoiding the main roads where refugees were being systematically hunted, crossing wilderness areas where wild animals posed less danger than human beings, constantly battling hunger and thirst while maintaining the appearance of a holy man on a pilgrimage, it took nine long weeks.

They walked by night when possible, hiding during the day in ruins, abandoned temples, or caves. They survived on whatever food they could beg from the few remaining Hindu communities they encountered, supplemented by wild fruits and whatever edible plants they could identify. Water came from streams and rain puddles, often contaminated but preferable to dying of thirst.

The physical hardships were nothing compared to the psychological trauma of witnessing the collapse of everything they had believed about human nature and civilized society. They saw things that no human being should see, encountered survivors whose stories defied belief, passed through places where the stench of death hung in the air like a permanent fog.

But they also witnessed acts of heroism and compassion that restored faith in humanity's capacity for good. Muslim families who risked their own lives to hide Hindu neighbors. Sikh truck drivers who made repeated trips into dangerous territory to evacuate refugees. British officials who disobeyed orders to help people escape. Random strangers who shared their last piece of bread with traveling monks.

When the group finally arrived in Delhi, they were barely recognizable as the men who had left Lahore. Sohan Lal's feet were cracked and bleeding, his body had been stripped of excess weight, and his face was hidden beneath a long beard that made him look like an ancient sage. But his eyes still held that characteristic twinkle.

To understand the philosophical framework that sustained Sohan Lal during his journey and would continue to guide him throughout his life, one must understand the depth and antiquity of the Vedic tradition that had shaped his worldview.

The Sanskrit word *Veda* means knowledge—not just any knowledge, but the deepest possible understanding of the relationship between consciousness and creation. The Vedas originated among the Indo-Aryan culture thousands of years ago and were passed down orally from guru to student with such precision that scholars consider them among the most accurately preserved texts in human history.

For countless generations, these teachings existed only in the minds and voices of trained priests and sages who could recite thousands of verses without error. Between 1500 and 500 BCE, this oral tradition was finally committed to writing in Sanskrit on palm leaves, creating a body of literature that would become the foundation for virtually every aspect of Indian civilization.

The ultimate origin of the Vedas is traced to the inhabitants of the Indus Valley civilization five thousand years ago, a sophisticated urban culture that flourished along the banks of the now-extinct river Saraswati in what is present-day Pakistan. This mighty river originated from the Himalayan peaks, flowed through the fertile Indus valley, and then merged with the Indian Ocean, creating a corridor of prosperity and wisdom that sustained millions of people.

The Vedic seers understood that individual consciousness and cosmic consciousness were not separate phenomena but different expressions of the same fundamental reality. This insight gave birth to an extraordinary range of sciences and practices: Ayurveda (the science of life and healing), *Jyotisha* (Vedic astronomy and astrology), Palmistry (the reading of cosmic influences through hand patterns), Yoga (the technology of union), Pranayama (breath regulation), Mantra (sound therapy), Mudra (sacred gestures), Yantra (geometric meditation tools), and Tantra (the path of transformation through embodiment).

These disciplines were understood to be beads on the necklace of Vedic wisdom, each offering a different method for fine-tuning the human form by connecting it with universal consciousness. All were based on the fundamental Vedic insight that every manifested form in the universe—from the tiniest atom to the largest galaxy—is composed of *Panch Tattvas*, the five elements: *Prithvi* (earth), *Apas* (water), *Agni* (fire), *Vayu* (air), and *Akasha* (ether).

When Sohan Lal arrived in Delhi in 1948, the ancient city had been transformed into something unprecedented in its long history: a vast refugee camp housing millions of displaced people. Delhi had always been a city of conquerors and refugees —it had been destroyed and rebuilt several times over the centuries, each iteration rising from the ashes of the previous one. But nothing in its past had prepared it for the human tsunami that was now washing over its walls.

The city was filled with the architectural remnants of its complex past: crumbling Mughal forts whose red sandstone and white marble walls had witnessed the rise and fall of empires, sprawling gardens where emperors had once composed poetry and planned conquests, luxurious mansions built by princes and merchants who had grown wealthy on the silk road trade, and the massive government buildings erected by the British to house their administrators and showcase the power of the Raj.

But now, every open space in the city had been transformed into temporary housing for refugees. Public parks where children had once played were packed with makeshift tents constructed from whatever materials people had been able to carry or scavenge. The beautiful Mughal gardens, designed as earthly representations of paradise, were filled with the cooking fires and clotheslines of families who had lost everything except each other.

The air was thick with smoke from thousands of cooking fires and something else—their silent screams for all that had been snatched from them, including family members who might never be found, created an almost tangible atmosphere of trauma that hung over the city like smog.

My father was fortunate to find temporary shelter in the heart of New Delhi at the Ramakrishna Mission, where all the monks who had made the journey from Lahore were housed. Jobs for educated refugees were scarce in a city already struggling to absorb millions of displaced people. The colonial economy had been designed to extract wealth from India to Britain, not to provide employment for Indians.

Entrepreneurship became not just an opportunity but a survival requirement. Within a couple of months of his arrival in Delhi, Sohan Lal had landed a position that seemed almost too good to be true: geography teacher at Modern School, one of the most prestigious educational institutions in the city. The school catered to children from primary through high school age, primarily the offspring of the fortunate and famous—the political leaders, successful businessmen, and cultural figures who were shaping the new nation.

The school was set amid rolling green lawns in one of Delhi's most desirable neighborhoods. As part of his compensation, he was allotted a small room in the boys' hostel in exchange for serving as housemaster—a position that required him to be both teacher and surrogate parent to students whose own parents were often too busy building the new nation to provide the guidance their children needed.

Finally, after several months of uncertainty, Sohan Lal had a stable postal address and could write to tell his family that he had not only survived but was beginning to rebuild his life. The letter he wrote home was brief—he was never one for elaborate emotional expression—but the mere fact of its existence was enough to restore his family's faith that their prayers had been answered.

The trauma of partition had created in him what psychologists would later recognize as a common response to survival: a determination to provide for his family that was so fierce it could overshadow other considerations, including the emotional needs of family members who had not shared his experiences.

CHAPTER 3
Susheila, the Songbird

In early 1947, as India trembled on the precipice of independence and partition, my mother Susheila turned sixteen in Hoshiarpur—a name that translates to "home of the vigilant." This ancient city in eastern Punjab would soon find itself on the Indian side of the newly drawn border, its Hindu and Sikh inhabitants remaining while Muslim families fled westward to the newly created Pakistan.

Within its dusty streets and weathered buildings lay some of the original Bhrigu writings, inscribed on palm leaves that had survived centuries. Here, Maharishi Bhrigu had composed the *Bhrigu Samhita*—an astrological treatise mapping the journey of individual souls from birth to death, cataloging the positive and negative karma destined for each life, the inevitable consequences, and the prescribed remedies to prevent undesirable karmic seeds from taking root.

Across the world, American psychic Edgar Cayce drew upon what he called "God's Book of Remembrance" during his trance states, believing that the past and future of all humanity resided in the sky above—a cosmic database known as the Akashic Records. This celestial archive, he claimed, held every action and thought of every soul who had ever walked the earth. *Akasha*—the Sanskrit word meaning "all-encompassing"—seemed fitting for such an infinite repository of human experience.

The name Susheila means "one of happy nature," and she embodied this meaning despite the turbulence that defined her childhood. She was indeed a people person, a songbird whose spirit yearned for open skies. The soundtrack of her early years was punctuated by her mother Vidyavati's wails and screams—sounds that would echo through the household whenever financial disaster struck.

Her father, Daulat Ram, was a study in contradictions. A prominent lawyer whose reputation commanded respect in Hoshiarpur's legal circles, he was also a compulsive gambler who treated the commodities market like his personal casino. As the sole provider for a family of ten—eight children plus their parents—his wins and losses created a household rhythm of feast or famine that left everyone perpetually uncertain about tomorrow's meals or next season's clothing.

Susheila occupied the precarious middle ground among her siblings: three sisters and four brothers. The smallpox that scarred her in childhood left several small dark marks on her cheeks—imperfections that seemed magnified in her own mind when compared to the prized, clear, wheatish complexions of her sisters. Sarla, five years her senior; Santosh, just a year younger; and Swaraj, the youngest. Susheila convinced herself she was the ugliest—a belief that would shape her determination to distinguish herself in other ways.

When Susheila completed high school, the path before her seemed predetermined. In their household—as in most traditional families of the time—education followed gender lines. Boys were encouraged to pursue college and professional careers. Girls were required to transition from middle school to the domestic arts: sewing with precision, singing with sweetness, and cooking with skill—all in service of pleasing future husbands and appeasing future in-laws.

When Susheila expressed her desire to continue her education, her mother's response was delivered with the blunt efficiency of a financial statement: "There is simply no money in the household budget for your college fees and books." The message was clear—her education was a luxury the family could not afford, especially when that money might be needed for her brothers' futures or her own eventual dowry.

But my mother possessed a stubborn streak that ran deeper than family tradition. She was determined not to end up "tied to the kitchen like her mother." Through a combination of persistence, pleading, and perhaps a well-timed moment when her father's gambling had yielded a windfall, she convinced Daulat Ram to find the money for her education.

For five years, Susheila rode a bicycle to the local branch of Punjab University. She studied economics—a subject that perhaps appealed to her practical nature, shaped as it was by years of witnessing the boom-and-bust cycles of her father's financial adventures. When she finally earned her master's degree, it became more than a qualification—it was her coveted possession, a feather in her cap that distinguished her from every other woman in her family. None of her sisters had studied past middle school, making her achievement both a source of pride and a subtle form of isolation.

At twenty-two, armed with her master's degree in economics like a shield, Susheila displayed a confidence that shocked her family. When a decent marriage proposal arrived—a respectable young man from a good family—she rejected it with an explanation that left her parents speechless: the prospective groom only had a bachelor's degree. Her education had given her not just knowledge, but the audacity to believe she deserved an equal match.

The irony was swift and cutting. A month later, her younger sister Santosh was married to the same man Susheila had deemed beneath her educational standards. All the money that had been saved for Susheila's dowry—the financial cushion that might have made her more attractive to potential suitors—was transferred to Santosh's marriage fund, leaving Susheila's prospects significantly diminished.

Months passed with increasing anxiety in the household. An unmarried daughter past twenty was a source of growing concern. Then salvation arrived in the form of a letter from

Rattan Singh, her eldest brother who had established himself in New Delhi. His message was brief but pregnant with possibility: "There is an interesting matrimonial ad in the *Hindustan Times*. Twenty-eight-year-old man of the same caste with master's degree in mathematics seeks an educated bride. There is no requirement of fair skin or dowry in this advertisement."

The absence of these two requirements—fair skin and dowry—was revolutionary. In a society where marriages were essentially financial transactions dressed up in religious ceremony, finding a groom who valued education over economics seemed like discovering a rare gem in a marketplace of stones.

On a predestined day, Susheila and Sohan Lal's futures were bound together in a Vedic fire ceremony that was remarkable more for its simplicity than its grandeur. The local priest tended the sacred fire while the bride and groom, their scarfs tied together in symbolic unity, completed seven circumambulations around the flames. According to ancient tradition, Agni—the fire element—would transport their desire for a blissful conjugal union to the Akasha element, where universal consciousness resided and cosmic records were kept. The fire element, believed to reside in the navel of all humans, served as the gateway between earthly existence and divine realms.

Notably absent from the wedding preparations was the traditional practice of comparing the bride and groom's *Janam Kundali*—their birth charts—for astrological compatibility. Susheila's parents were too relieved to have found any suitable groom to concern themselves with celestial approval. Their focus had already shifted to the next challenge: finding a husband for their next daughter in line.

With two metal trunks containing her worldly possessions, wide-eyed Susheila arrived in New Delhi, the bustling capital that represented modernity and opportunity. Her first glimpse of her new life was sobering. Despite his impressive educational credentials, Sohan Lal lived in conditions that could only be described as monastic.

The sparse dowry that accompanied Susheila became an immediate source of tension. When Sohan Lal's mother came to visit and inventory her new daughter-in-law's contributions to the household, her shock was palpable and her displeasure poorly concealed. Instead of basking in the traditional honeymoon phase of arranged marriage—where couples were expected to grow into love gradually—Susheila and Sohan Lal found themselves arguing about money.

Sohan Lal made his priorities crystal clear with the directness of a dutiful son: his obligations to his aging parents and his responsibility to save for his younger sister's wedding took precedence over any romantic notions about married life. For Susheila, who had sacrificed her dowry to her sister's marriage and now found herself in a union where financial pragmatism trumped emotional connection, the reality of her situation must have felt like a cruel repetition of her childhood's feast-or-famine cycles.

But Susheila had not endured five years of university education to become a passive participant in her own life. A couple of months into their marriage, with a decisiveness that would characterize her approach to obstacles throughout her life, she announced her intention to earn teaching credentials. This decision required her to leave Delhi for an entire year, living in the dormitory of an all-women's college in another city.

Upon her return to Delhi, armed with her teaching qualifications, Susheila secured a position teaching first grade at Modern School, the same institution where her husband taught high school students. This professional partnership marked the beginning of their transformation from reluctant spouses to collaborative partners. The couple moved from their cramped single room to a two-bedroom flat and hired domestic help—luxury that their combined incomes now made possible.

Slowly, like flowers that bloom only after the harshest winter, their romance began to blossom. The shared experience of professional life, the gradual accumulation of modest prosperity, and perhaps simply the passage of time allowed affection to take root where only obligation had existed before. Their relationship flowered into something that resembled the marriages of choice they had observed in others—built on mutual respect, shared goals, and growing fondness.

Three years into their marriage, at another predestined moment, Susheila delivered a baby girl in the local hospital under the care of Western medicine—a choice that represented their embrace of modernity over tradition. They named their daughter Anjali, a name meaning "offering."

But even as their personal life stabilized, Susheila's ambitions reached beyond the boundaries of domestic contentment. She recognized that her husband's talents were being underutilized in the Indian educational system and persuaded him to apply for a scholarship to study abroad. When Sohan Lal was accepted at Ohio State University, the opportunity came with a devastating choice: he could afford to support himself for one year of study, but not his wife and six-month-old daughter.

The decision required Susheila to demonstrate once again the resilience that had carried her through childhood poverty and educational barriers. She gave up everything she had carefully crafted and assembled since her marriage to a stranger three and a half years earlier—their Delhi flat, her teaching position, their hired help, their professional partnership, their hard-won independence.

Cradling six-month-old Anjali, she boarded a train with a single suitcase, leaving behind the cosmopolitan capital for Patiala in Punjab, where she would spend the next year under the watchful and critical eye of her mother-in-law.

The year that followed tested every aspect of Susheila's character. In her mother-in-law's household, her master's degree in economics meant nothing. Her teaching credentials carried no weight. Her professional accomplishments were invisible, irrelevant to the daily requirements of Vedic rituals and traditional domestic duties. She found herself criticized constantly for her failure to perform religious ceremonies with the expertise her mother-in-law had spent decades perfecting. She had no friends in this new city, no professional identity to anchor her sense of self, no escape from the relentless scrutiny of a woman who viewed her daughter-in-law's modern education as evidence of improper priorities.

Adding to her isolation and stress, infant Anjali struggled with one illness after another, requiring constant care and creating additional worry. The contrast between her previous life—teaching first-graders, managing a household with hired help, living as an equal partner in a dual-career marriage—and her current existence as a dependent daughter-in-law must have been almost unbearable.

When my father returned from the United States with his postgraduate degree in Audio-Visual Education, he brought with him not just enhanced qualifications but access to opportunities that would transform their lives once again. He was selected for a managerial position in the emerging field of audio-visual education, a role created by the Ministry of Education in New Delhi as India modernized its educational infrastructure. Simultaneously, my mother secured a position as a medical social worker in the Ministry of Health, specifically focused on promoting family planning—work that aligned with India's growing awareness of population challenges.

Within months, they had joined the ranks of up-and-coming civil servants in New Delhi, beneficiaries of a newly independent nation's investment in education and public health. The Indian government allocated my father a spacious bungalow at 3-B Bangla Sahib Lane, located in a prestigious neighborhood. The house itself carried historical weight—built in the early 1900s for the pleasure of British civil servants who had once managed Indian affairs from these same rooms.

For my younger sister Sadhana whose features resembled my mom but with a flawless wheatish complexion and me, this bungalow became the backdrop for countless games of hide-and-seek, our laughter echoing through spaces that had once hosted the conversations of colonial administrators. The spacious lawn and surrounding gardens provided a playground that reflected our family's ascent into India's emerging middle class—a class that would define the country's post-independence identity.

CHAPTER 4
Gaura Devi, My Look-Alike

The name of my paternal grandmother, Gaura Devi, is synonymous with the goddess Parvati, the divine consort of Shiva and the embodiment of feminine power in its most nurturing form. Her mother, Ganeshi Devi, was named after Parvati's mind-born son Ganesha, the beloved elephant-headed deity who removes obstacles from the path toward spiritual and physical balance. In the intricate architecture of Vedic rituals, no ceremony begins without first invoking Ganesha's blessings, acknowledging his role as the guardian of thresholds and the remover of impediments that block the harmonious flow of the five elements within the human body-mind complex.

Gaura Devi's physical presence was striking in its understated elegance. Her skin held the warm, rich tone of freshly ground cinnamon. Her medium-sized frame carried no excess weight. Her long, tapered fingers and feet suggested an inherent grace, while her arched black eyebrows framed brown eyes that held depths of experience.

Those eyes—pools of mystery that seemed to contain lifetimes of unspoken stories—dominated her face, leading to a long and elegant nose pierced on the left side with a simple round silver pin. This single adornment honored the feminine aspect of her being, following ancient traditions that recognized the left side of the body as the lunar, receptive channel. Her eyes held more expression than her mouth ever did; she had learned early that emotional displays were luxuries she could not afford.

Gaura Devi's approach to life was fundamentally pragmatic,

rooted in ancestral wisdom passed down through generations of women who understood that survival often depended on intimate knowledge of nature's healing properties. She relied on her collection of spices and the lunar-based rituals inherited from her foremothers to address everything that ailed her family. Her inner yearnings found relief through the performance of intricate ceremonies timed to the moon's phases, each ritual designed to align her personal energy with the cosmic rhythms that governed all life.

Perhaps most tellingly, Gaura Devi never celebrated Diwali—the Festival of Lights that illuminates India with joy and anticipation each year. On the darkest night of the waning new moon, typically falling between late October and early November, millions of devotees light countless clay lamps and prepare elaborate sweet offerings for Lakshmi, the goddess of abundance and the fulfillment of desires. Dressed in their finest clothing, families throughout India fling open their front doors and windows, beckoning the divine feminine energy to enter their homes and bless their households with prosperity.

The iconography of Lakshmi is both beautiful and symbolically rich. She stands serenely atop a red lotus—the flower that rises pure from muddy waters, representing the soul's ability to transcend material circumstances. Her open eyes radiate compassion while her mouth curves in the gentle smile of divine grace. Adorned with elaborate ear ornaments and necklaces of precious jewels and gold, she wears a pristine white sari with a red blouse.

Lakshmi's four hands tell the story of divine abundance: her upper hands hold pink lotus buds representing spiritual unfoldment, while her lower right hand forms the sacred mudra of granting boons—a gesture where the elbow stays close to the body, the forearm extends at a right angle, and the open palm faces outward with four fingers straight and the thumb positioned at a forty-five-degree angle. From her lower left hand, which points downward in the gesture of giving, golden coins flow endlessly, symbolizing the divine source of all material abundance.

Two white elephants, symbols of wisdom and fortune, stand guard on either side of the goddess, their trunks adorned with garlands of marigolds. Astrologically, Venus is appeased through prayers to Lakshmi, as this planet governs both material and spiritual desires within an individual's birth chart, influencing one's capacity to attract beauty, love, and abundance.

But for Gaura Devi, Diwali would forever be associated with tragedy rather than celebration. When she was six years old, her three-year-old brother's soul was claimed by Yama Dev, the lord of death, on a Diwali night. The cause was a fireworks explosion. The festival that brought light to others brought only darkness to her family.

A year after her brother's death, when Gaura Devi was seven, her grieving father passed away, his spirit apparently broken by the loss of his young son. The double blow of losing both her brother and father in such quick succession left an indelible mark on her understanding of life's fragility and the suddenness with which everything could change.

Following the cultural expectations of her time, Gaura Devi completed sixth grade at the local girls' school before her formal education ended. From that point forward, her curriculum consisted of the domestic arts deemed essential for her future role as wife and mother: cooking techniques passed down through generations, sewing skills that would clothe her family, and the complex rituals needed to properly honor and appease the mother goddess.

When Gaura Devi reached twenty, another tragedy struck with devastating force. Her widowed mother, Ganeshi Devi, was murdered under circumstances that remained shrouded in mystery and family secrecy. By this time, Gaura Devi was already married to Kundan Lal and had given birth to her five-year-old son, Sohan Lal—my father. The details of her mother's death were rarely discussed, with my grandmother limiting her comments to the repeated assertion that "her mother was a very brave woman."

The full story of Ganeshi Devi's death remained hidden until three decades after Gaura Devi's own passing. Only then did my father's youngest brother, Bhagwat Dutt, share the family's dark secret with me. His account revealed a tragedy rooted in the intersection of property rights, gender vulnerability, and family honor:

"Upon the birth of her grandson Sohan Lal," he told me, "Ganeshi Devi—your great-grandmother, then a thirty-six-year-old widow—committed what her in-laws considered a grave transgression. She traveled alone to the heavily guarded mansion of her extremely wealthy in-laws, determined to secure her deceased husband's share of the family property for her grandson's future."

"The next morning," Bhagwat Dutt continued, his voice heavy with old pain, "her lifeless body, wrapped in a white cotton shroud, was deposited on her brother's doorstep. It was declared a matter of family honor—no police report was filed, no postmortem was requested, no investigation was pursued. Her body was quickly consumed by the hungry flames at the local cremation grounds, and her soul departed to the astral realms carrying unresolved issues that would hang forever in her loved ones' hearts."

This brutal end to Ganeshi Devi's life reveals the dangerous territory that women of her generation navigated when they dared to assert legal or property rights. As the oldest child of a renowned and wealthy family in Patiala, she had been raised with every advantage her society could offer a female child. Various tutors had made her proficient in singing, writing, sewing, and fine cooking—accomplishments that marked her as a woman of refinement and culture. She had followed her mother's example.

At fifteen, she had been married to an eligible man from a family of similar social and economic status—an arrangement that should have secured her position and protection for life. Gaura Devi was born when Ganeshi Devi was just sixteen.

The scope of loss that defined Gaura Devi's life becomes even more staggering when viewed chronologically. By the time she reached thirty-two, she had given birth to five children, with Bhagwat Dutt being the youngest—seventeen years younger than my father, Sohan Lal. When Gaura Devi turned thirty-seven, another devastating blow struck: her son Indrajeet died at the age of thirteen after contracting smallpox, a disease that killed swiftly and without mercy.

This loss shattered something fundamental in Kundan Lal, Gaura Devi's husband. According to family lore, his hair turned completely white overnight—a physical manifestation of grief so profound that it literally altered his body. From that point forward, he became increasingly detached from worldly concerns.

Two years later, in 1947, the political upheaval of Partition forced the family to confront loss on an entirely different scale. For months, they had held onto hope that their hometown of Pindi Bhattian would be allocated to India rather than Pakistan, allowing them to remain in the place that had been their home for twenty years. When the final borders were drawn and their worst fears were realized, they faced the same terrible choice confronting millions of families across the subcontinent: flee or die.

They left with only the clothes on their backs, joining the massive human rivers of refugees flowing in both directions across the newly created border. Gaura Devi, with the practical wisdom born of multiple losses, stuffed her gold jewelry into the lining of her undergarments. Her husband secured their home's front door with a heavy iron lock, maintaining the illusion that this departure might be temporary, unaware that everything they left behind was lost to them forever. The family made their way to their ancestral home in Patiala, India.

By the time Gaura Devi reached sixty-four, she had witnessed the deaths of six beloved family members: her three-year-old brother lost to a fireworks accident, her father who died of grief, her courageous mother murdered for asserting property rights, her adolescent son claimed by smallpox, her seventy-two-year-old husband worn down by accumulated sorrows, and finally, her firstborn son Sohan Lal—my father—who departed for the astral realms without warning at the seemingly arbitrary age of forty-seven.

I was nine years old when my grandmother became a permanent part of our household, arriving after her youngest child, Bhagwat Dutt, followed in his eldest brother's footsteps and traveled to the United States for further studies.

By this time in her life, Gaura Devi could not fully extend her right arm due to an unattended fracture at the elbow that had healed improperly. The arm remained bent at a forty-five-degree angle. She required assistance lifting heavy objects, but the long, flexible fingers of her compromised right hand retained enough dexterity to adjust the muslin scarf that always covered her head and to braid her white hair into a single, neat plait that hung down her back like a silver rope.

Unlike most Indian women of her generation, who adorned themselves with bangles that chimed softly as they moved, earrings that caught the light, and necklaces that marked their marital status and family wealth, Gaura Devi wore no jewelry whatsoever.

Her wardrobe reflected this same austere aesthetic: three pairs of light-colored salwar kameez and white dupatta—simple, functional clothing that could be easily washed and required no special care.

Despite her avoidance of Diwali, Gaura Devi found deep meaning in Navratri—the nine nights of the year specifically reserved for honoring Shakti, the divine feminine principle that underlies all creation. This festival preceded Diwali by a fortnight and began during the waxing stage of the new moon.

Each of the nine nights of Navratri honored a different aspect of the goddess. The culmination came on the tenth night, Vijaya Dashami, when Ma Durga—a fierce incarnation of Shakti—triumphed over the mythical demon Mahishasura, representing the victory of divine consciousness over ignorance and evil.

For Gaura Devi, the most meaningful aspect of Navratri was the tradition of cooking a special meal for nine prepubescent girls, a practice that honored the divine feminine principle in its purest, most innocent form. It became my job to round up these young participants from our neighborhood.

The ritual itself was elaborate and deeply symbolic. Each girl would have her feet ceremonially washed by my grandmother—an act of reverence that acknowledged the divine presence within each child. Then a red thread would be tied around each girl's right wrist, creating a protective barrier against negative influences. Finally, the feast would be served: halwa (a sweet confection), puri (deep-fried bread), and channa (spiced chickpeas), all prepared with ghee and served on banana leaves.

My participation in this ceremony ended abruptly when I reached eleven and began menstruating. According to the traditional beliefs that governed my grandmother's spiritual practice, my transition from girl to woman meant I could no longer represent the pure, prepubescent energy that the ritual required.

Of all the possessions that Gaura Devi had been forced to abandon in Pakistan during Partition, the one I most longed to experience was her spice box. Though I never laid eyes on this legendary container, my imagination conjured it in vivid detail based on her descriptions. In my mind's eye, I could see this masterpiece of functional art: a handcrafted circular box of glowing beaten brass, its surface burnished to a warm golden sheen by generations of use.

The design was both practical and beautiful, with a tight-fitting lid topped by a round knob in its center that served as a handle.

Inside, the box was divided like a mandala, with a central silver cup surrounded by eight smaller compartments, each designed to hold a different spice. The central cup was always filled with ground turmeric root—her most beloved and frequently used spice.

Through this spice box, my tongue could travel to distant lands on clouds of flavor and fragrance. Yellow turmeric provided earthiness and healing properties. Black pepper offered heat and circulation-enhancing qualities. Brown cumin and coriander seeds contributed nutty, warm notes that grounded heavier dishes. Dark brown cloves, cinnamon, and nutmeg brought sweetness and preservation qualities that extended beyond the merely culinary. Small green cardamom pods held floral, almost perfumed essences, while larger black cardamom provided smoky depth that seemed to contain the memory of ancient fires.

The reality of our Delhi kitchen was humbler. The spice box my grandmother used there was mass-produced rather than handcrafted—a simple rectangular wooden container with a loose-fitting lid that slid back and forth to reveal six basic compartments.

Each morning, Gaura Devi's day began with a ritual that connected her to both her body and the earth's abundance. After drinking a glass of lukewarm water from a copper tumbler—a practice that honored Ayurvedic principles about proper hydration and the healing properties of copper—she would squat on the cement floor of our kitchen next to the coal and mud cooker to knead fresh wheat dough.

Even with her compromised right arm, she managed to create minor miracles of texture and flavor. Using her functional left hand in coordination with her partially disabled right, she fashioned flaky, multi-layered parathas that seemed to contain layers of air and butter in perfect proportion. These were cooked with ghee until they achieved the ideal balance of crispy exterior and tender interior, then served to me with fresh yogurt and tangy mango pickle, the entire meal washed down with sips of perfectly spiced masala chai.

Her relationship with ginger bordered on the reverential. She would peel the brown skin from ginger root with meticulous care, ensuring that none of the prized nutrients lying just beneath the surface were disturbed or wasted. Her tribute to this remarkable root could be translated as: "Only the wise recognize the curative traits of ginger; a monkey takes a bite and spits it out"—a saying that captured both the spice's powerful, sometimes challenging flavor and the wisdom required to appreciate its healing properties.

Most of the spices in Gaura Devi's arsenal were kept in their whole seed form, preserving their essential oils and potency until the moment of use. The two exceptions to this rule were ginger and turmeric—the king and queen of her spice kingdom. Both of these remarkable plants propagate through their underground root systems while producing captivating but sterile flowers above ground.

Gaura Devi's approach to food was guided by Ayurvedic principles, particularly the concept of the three gunas—the fundamental attributes that categorize all matter and energy in the universe. She practiced this ancient wisdom with the precision of a scientist and the intuition of a mystic, understanding that food was medicine and medicine was food.

She taught me that all consumable matter belongs to one of three categories known in Sanskrit as Tri Guna: Sattva represents clarity, purity, and light; Rajas embodies activity, passion, and movement; while Tamas encompasses heaviness, inertia, and darkness. According to this system, the roots of a plant are considered tamasic—grounding but potentially dulling if consumed in excess. The leaves and stems are rajasic—energizing and activating. The seeds, fruits, and flowers are sattvic—promoting clarity, spiritual awareness, and harmonious balance.

Gaura Devi consumed only sattvic and rajasic foods, carefully avoiding anything that might increase tamasic energy in her system.

When I developed sniffles or showed signs of respiratory congestion, she would promptly slice ginger root into paper-thin pieces and fry them in ghee until they became light brown and aromatic. Then she would sprinkle brown sugar on top, transforming the fiery root into something my young palate could willingly accept. The combination of ginger's warming properties, ghee's nourishing qualities, and sugar's immediate energy created a medicine that worked on multiple levels simultaneously.

For cuts, scrapes, or any skin irritation, she would create a healing paste from turmeric root powder and ghee, slathering this golden mixture onto my skin with the confidence of someone who had witnessed its effectiveness countless times. The turmeric provided antiseptic and anti-inflammatory properties, while the ghee served as both carrier and moisturizer.

On school exam days, when my stomach churned with nervous energy, she would prepare a special yogurt mixture topped with carefully measured amounts of salt, black pepper, and sugar. This seemingly simple preparation actually represented sophisticated knowledge of how to calm the digestive fire that resides in the stomach. The yogurt provided cooling probiotics, the salt replaced electrolytes, the black pepper stimulated digestion, and the sugar offered immediate energy for my nervous system. Before stepping out the front door to face my examinations, I would happily consume this healing mixture.

CHAPTER 5
Hanuman the Divine Helper

By age nine, the boundary between sleep and waking had become a war zone where shadowy figures pursued me through labyrinthine dreams, their faces shifting and blurring, just beyond recognition yet somehow terrifyingly familiar. I would bolt upright in the pre-dawn darkness, my small body drenched in cold sweat, palms clammy and heart hammering against my ribs like a caged bird desperate for freedom. The terror didn't end with waking—it followed me into the daylight hours, clinging to my skin like an invisible shroud.

During the day, I moved through our Delhi home like a child carrying a terrible secret, attempting to ignore the ghosts of guilt that seemed to wrap themselves around my shoulders. The weight was unbearable for a nine-year-old, this sense that I was somehow fundamentally flawed, marked by sins I couldn't even remember committing.

The inner voice that had become my constant, unwelcome companion offered its relentless analysis: "Anjali, you must be cursed from your past life. Why else would you suffer so much when other children seem so carefree?"

I tried to ignore it, but the voice persisted with the ruthless logic of childhood's attempt to make sense of inexplicable suffering: "You must have committed several terrible sins in past lives. Search your memory—do you recall hurting anyone in this life? There must be some explanation for why happiness seems to slip through your fingers like water."

The burden of this cosmic guilt was crushing. In a worldview where every action ripples across lifetimes, where karma accumulates like spiritual debt, a child's suffering could only mean one thing: I was paying for crimes I couldn't even remember. The injustice of this felt overwhelming, yet it also provided a strange comfort—at least there was a reason for my pain, even if that reason lay buried in the mists of previous incarnations.

Salvation came in an unexpected form. Based on the wise cockatiel's advice—which I had come to trust as there was no one I could confide in—I embarked upon memorizing the Hanuman Chalisa, forty verses dedicated to Hanuman, the monkey god who embodied unwavering devotion, supernatural strength, and the power to overcome seemingly impossible obstacles. The prescription was precise and demanding: these verses were to be chanted 108 times each day.

Hanuman's iconography spoke to something deep in my troubled spirit. Unlike the other gods and goddesses who could be depicted with multiple arms—sometimes four, six, or even ten hands depending upon the complexity of their cosmic responsibilities—Hanuman possessed the elegant simplicity of two hands set upon a powerful human torso, crowned by the intelligent, expressive face of a monkey. This combination of human and animal seemed to bridge the civilized and the wild, the rational and the instinctual, offering a kind of divine accessibility that the other deities lacked.

His fifth limb—a maneuverable tail that aided in balance while flying through the skies and bounding up mountains—represented the extra capability that devotion could provide, the additional strength that came from complete surrender to divine will. In artistic depictions, his raised left hand typically held a saffron flag, the color of renunciation and spiritual commitment, while his right gripped a mace symbolizing the power to destroy negativity. His stance was both grounded and dynamic: his right foot planted firmly on the earth, his left foot resting atop a mountain one-third his size, suggesting mastery over the material world.

I began making regular visits to an ancient temple dedicated to Hanuman, located a twenty-minute walk from our home through the bustling streets of Delhi. This temple carried extraordinary historical weight—it was said to have been erected during the times of Lord Krishna himself, making it over five thousand years old according to traditional chronology. The very stones seemed to pulse with accumulated prayers and centuries of devotional energy.

Inside the temple's inner sanctum stood an aboriginal likeness of Hanuman crafted from yellowish stone, its surface perpetually smeared with red powder—sindoor applied by countless devotees seeking strength and courage. According to temple lore, this sacred structure had been commissioned by the five Pandava brothers at the conclusion of the legendary Kurukshetra war, as chronicled in the epic Mahabharata, to thank Hanuman for his crucial assistance in their victory against their own cousins in that cosmic battle between dharma and adharma.

The story of that war, preserved in the Bhagavad Gita, held particular significance for my nine-year-old struggles with duty and fear. Written in Sanskrit, this sacred text narrates the dialogue between Shri Krishna and Arjuna—one of the five Pandava brothers and the greatest archer of his generation—on the battlefield of Kurukshetra. When Arjuna surveyed the opposing army and recognized his beloved archery teacher and revered great-grandfather among the enemy ranks, his warrior's resolve crumbled like a sandcastle before the tide.

Krishna, serving as his charioteer but revealing himself as the divine incarnation, counseled Arjuna about dharma—the cosmic principle of righteous duty that transcends personal preference and emotional attachment. Krishna's teaching was revolutionary in its simplicity and devastating in its demands: "Your duty is to fight without giving any consideration to the outcome; only then will you be able to find moksha, or freedom from the mental fluctuations that create suffering."

According to Vedic wisdom, human life unfolds through four distinct stages, each building upon the previous one:

Dharma: Finding your duty, your purpose—the unique role you are meant to play in the cosmic drama

Artha: Gathering the resources, skills, and knowledge necessary to accomplish your dharma

Kama: The joy and fulfillment derived from completing your duty with excellence and devotion

Moksha: Freedom from desires and fears, the blissful state of union with divine consciousness

Every Tuesday—the day of the week presided over by Hanuman's fierce energy—the temple transformed into something resembling a carnival. A mela, or festive gathering, would spontaneously emerge outside the temple grounds, drawing devotees and curious tourists from across Delhi. Street vendors lined the approaches to the temple, their colorful stalls offering an intoxicating array of savory snacks, sweet treats, and handcrafted wares created by artisans from nearby villages who saw the weekly gathering as both spiritual pilgrimage and economic opportunity.

On summer evenings, as office workers and laborers made their way home through Delhi's sweltering heat, streams of impatient devotees would converge on the temple entrance, pushing and jostling with the urgency of people carrying heavy burdens they desperately needed to set down. They pressed into the inner sanctum, each person seeking that moment of direct contact with the divine—the privilege of smearing red powder on Hanuman's stone forehead with their right ring finger, a gesture that would transfer the god's legendary strength and perseverance into their own struggling hearts.

The rhythmic chanting of the Hanuman Chalisa created a sonic backdrop that seemed to vibrate in my bones, the ancient Sanskrit syllables carrying meanings that transcended intellectual understanding. The smell of clarified butter—ghee burned in oil lamps—mingled with the earthy scent of human sweat and devotion, creating an olfactory signature that I would forever associate with the presence of the sacred. The sticky feels of gray marble under my bare feet, worn smooth by millions of pilgrims. And always, the sweet taste of prasad —blessed food distributed to devotees—lingered on my tongue like a promise that divine grace could be as tangible as sugar dissolving in saliva.

In those moments when I found myself face to face with the smiling stone visage of Hanuman; something shifted in my chest. The crushing weight of cosmic guilt would lift, replaced by a sensation I had almost forgotten existed: the feeling that I was being heard, understood, and unconditionally accepted by a consciousness.

My favorite vendor occupied a prime position near the temple entrance. This was an elderly man whose bald head was crowned by a saffron turban that had seen better decades, its fabric faded and frayed. A white beard hung from his weathered chin and his mouth was perpetually engaged in a toothless smile that suggested he possessed access to some cosmic joke that made all worldly concerns seem insignificant. The gray pupils in his sunken eyes seemed to emit actual rays of hope.

But the true star of his operation was his pet cockatiel, a creature who possessed what could only be described as paranormal powers despite appearing to be an ordinary bird. She displayed the classic cockatiel coloring: a bright yellow face marked by distinctive red dots on both cheeks, and a tail of elegant grayish feathers. What made her extraordinary was not her appearance but her uncanny ability to peer directly into the souls of visitors and select precisely the guidance they needed.

The old man's setup was deliberately simple, almost austere in its sacred geometry. In front of his cross-legged position, with the cockatiel perched regally on his left shoulder, lay a rectangular piece of homespun white cotton cloth that

CHAPTER 5

remained mysteriously unsullied by the dust and grime that coated everything else in the temple vicinity. At the center of this cloth sat a neat stack of well-worn, grayish index cards that looked identical when viewed from above—plain on one side, inscribed with three lines of black Hindi script on the other.

The ritual never varied, yet somehow it never became routine. After I placed my twenty-five paisa coin into his weathered palm—a sum that represented significant sacrifice from my small allowance—the old man would produce a distinctive clicking sound with his tongue and throat. This was a signal that activated the cockatiel's supernatural abilities, because she would immediately leap down from his shoulder and begin her deliberate approach toward the stack of cards.

Sometimes she moved with decisive purpose, hopping directly to her selection. Other times, she would pace back and forth in front of the row of cards like a scholar carefully considering weighty alternatives, her small head tilting from side to side. Always, she would raise her red crown feathers to full display before making her choice, using her curved yellow beak to extract one card from the stack with surgical precision.

The chosen card would be retrieved from the cockatiel's beak with the old man's left hand while his right simultaneously reached into the folds of his turban to produce a small treat for the bird—a reward for services rendered to the cosmos. Then he would read the selected message aloud in Hindi.

Each of the twenty-seven cards contained different advice, addressing the various forms of suffering and seeking that brought pilgrims to Hanuman's feet. There were cards about patience during difficult times, guidance for making important decisions, remedies for physical ailments, and strategies for overcoming family conflicts. Yet somehow, no matter how many times I consulted this mystical cockatiel, she invariably selected the same card for my particular predicament: "Keep on persevering and trust in Hanuman to drive away mountains of fear."

How did this seemingly ordinary bird possess such insight into my specific needs? How did she understand that fear had become the mountain blocking my path to happiness? And how did she know that by praying to Hanuman, the planet Mars in my astrological birth chart would be strengthened, imbuing me with the courage and perseverance?

According to Vedic astrology, Mars represents the warrior energy within each of us—the capacity to face challenges with courage, to persist through obstacles with determination, and to defend what is sacred with unwavering commitment.

Most visits to the temple mela required careful budgeting of my limited resources. After paying for the cockatiel's consultation, I rarely had enough money remaining to indulge in the colorful, spicy, sweet, and sour treats hawked by the food vendors, or to purchase the girlish accessories that caught my eye—delicate metal bangles that chimed musically when worn, garish earrings that caught the light like tiny stars, or colored plastic dots designed to decorate the forehead in imitation of the traditional tilak.

CHAPTER 6
Saraswati Devi, Goddess of Learning

Sohan Lal had grand aspirations for his daughters. When he enrolled both girls at Lady Irwin School, he chose one of Delhi's most prestigious all-girls institutions—a place where education was revered almost as sacred duty. Though the school bore the name of a long-departed British dignitary, there was nothing colonial about its spirit. "Saraswati Abode"—home of the goddess of learning—would have been a far more fitting name for this temple of knowledge.

Lady Irwin School stood apart from other institutions, and not merely because of its academic reputation. Under the bold leadership of Mrs. Sengupta, the headstrong, quirky principal who had taken the radical step of abandoning school uniforms—a practice rigidly maintained by every other school in Delhi—the institution pulsed with a different energy. Mrs. Sengupta was a formidable woman: stout and middle-aged, a widow whose bright gray eyes, magnified behind black-rimmed glasses, seemed to catalog every detail of her domain. Her daily uniform of white cotton sari and blouse spoke of simplicity, yet she encouraged her students to express themselves through colorful, modest clothing that reflected their individual personalities. In her world, conformity took a backseat to character.

"Address each other as 'sister' when you don't know a name," she would instruct, her voice carrying the weight of someone who understood that learning extended far beyond textbooks. This wasn't mere formality—it was her way of fostering sisterhood among girls who came from vastly different backgrounds, united by their shared pursuit of knowledge.

Of all the festivals that marked the Indian calendar—dozens of celebrations honoring various deities throughout the year—Mrs. Sengupta selected just one for the school's official observance. The festival of Vasant Panchami, dedicated to Saraswati, the goddess of learning and music, was celebrated with such enthusiasm that classes were suspended for the entire day. This wasn't simply a cultural gesture; it was a declaration of values, an acknowledgment that wisdom and creativity deserved their own sacred time.

Vasant Panchami arrives each year like a promise of renewal, falling on the fifth day of the waxing moon in early spring. Saraswati is recognized as another incarnation of Shakti—that primordial female energy that Hindus believe courses through all creation, the divine feminine force that brings forth life, knowledge, and transformation.

The festival day at Lady Irwin School unfolded like a carefully choreographed dance between tradition and youthful exuberance. While a benevolent sun cast its warmth from above and gentle breezes whispered through the sprawling campus grounds, girls would emerge from their classrooms transformed. Released from the ordinary constraints of daily routine, they moved across the grounds like vibrant butterflies, their specially chosen outfits a riot of colors and patterns that showcased personal style and cultural pride.

At the heart of the celebration stood a magnificent five-foot clay idol of Saraswati, positioned on a decorated pedestal in the center of the school grounds. The goddess's wheatish complexion seemed to glow against the backdrop of fresh green banana leaves arranged in intricate lattice patterns behind her. The ground beneath the idol became a living carpet of devotion—bright orange marigolds and sweet-smelling white jasmine scattered in generous profusion, their fragrance rising in the warm air and creating a sensory experience for the feet as well as the nose.

The spiritual significance of this worship ran deeper than mere ritual. Devotees believe that praying to Saraswati stimulates the intellect and enhances manifestation abilities—qualities represented in Vedic astrology by the planet Mercury. For students, this connection held special meaning: the goddess who governed learning and wisdom could enhance their capacity to absorb knowledge and express themselves with clarity and creativity.

Each girl would approach the idol individually, bowing at the goddess's feet to murmur her personal plea—perhaps for success in examinations, for clarity in understanding difficult concepts, or for the courage to pursue her dreams. Meanwhile, those waiting in line behind her would find their ears filled with the deep, resonant sound of conch shells being blown by the ceremony's officiants. The heat from twelve clay lamps surrounding the idol—each representing one of the zodiac signs—would cause beads of perspiration to form on the girls' foreheads. These lamps, filled with ghee and glowing from cotton wicks, created a circle of golden light that seemed to bring the stone idol to life.

Saraswati Ma herself was depicted in the traditional pose that has inspired devotees for millennia: seated in lotus position atop a pristine white lotus flower, with an elegant white swan positioned at her left side. The goddess's face radiated serenity and joy, her eyes closed in musical rapture, her smile suggesting the deep satisfaction that comes from perfect harmony between knowledge and artistic expression.

Her four arms each held symbolic significance. The upper left hand delicately fingered the strings of a sitar, its long neck extending gracefully upward, while the lower left hand palm leaf manuscripts. —representing the marriage of artistic creativity with scholarly learning. Her lower right hand rested supportively on the sitar's round base, grounding the music in practical skill, while her upper right hand held a mala—

a sacred necklace of 108 beads that carried profound spiritual significance.

The number 108 itself represents the mathematical perfection underlying Hindu cosmology: it is the product of the twenty-seven nakshatras (lunar mansions) multiplied by the nine planets recognized in Vedic astrology. Throughout the year, as the sun traces its elliptical path across the sky, it passes through these twenty-seven nakshatras, which divide the celestial sphere into distinct segments. Each of the twelve zodiac signs contains exactly two and a half nakshatras, creating a precise cosmic framework that influences human consciousness and physical well-being.

These twenty-seven-star groupings form recognizable patterns in the night sky, each believed to exert its own unique influence on human affairs. All Vedic festival dates are calculated based on the moon's position relative to these nakshatras, creating a calendar that aligns earthly celebrations with cosmic rhythms. The Sanskrit word "nakshatra" itself means "indestructible," suggesting that these stellar influences represent eternal principles that transcend the temporary concerns of daily life.

Among my most vivid memories from that time is a black-and-white class photograph taken on a clear, warm May morning, just days before the end of my eighth year. The image remains etched in my memory with startling clarity: twenty-two girls and our teacher, Miss Stephens, posed against a stone wall with bright sunlight streaming from behind and an emerald, green lawn stretching before us.

In the back row, eight girls stand in a neat line, with Miss Stephens towering a full head above even the tallest student. The middle row features seven girls kneeling formally, their arms positioned at their sides. The front row shows seven more girls sitting cross-legged on the ground, creating a pyramid of youthful faces arranged for posterity.

Picture day had inspired everyone to present their best selves. Hair was carefully combed and styled—the girls with shorter

CHAPTER 6

cuts wore theirs neatly trimmed and parted, while those with longer locks had woven colorful ribbons through their shining black hair. The range of expressions captured in that single moment reveals the complex inner worlds of these young women: some wore serious, thoughtful faces, others displayed tentative half-smiles, each girl navigating her own relationship with the camera and the formality of the occasion.

But it is one girl who draws my attention decades later. In the very center of the photograph, positioned in the second row of kneeling girls with three classmates on either side, sits this girl who stands apart from all the others. She is neither serious nor smiling. Instead, her lips are pursed in an expression that seems to contain multitudes—perhaps defiance, perhaps resignation, perhaps something more complicated than either. Her hair, unlike the carefully groomed locks of her classmates, appears uncombed, hastily tied back with several rebellious strands floating around her ears and forehead.

Miss Stephens herself presents a study in contrasts within the frame. Her long, chiseled nose and deep, compassionate eyes suggest someone who sees beyond surface appearances, while her serious mouth hints at the gravity with which she approaches her calling as an educator. Her skinny frame is draped in the simple cotton sari and blouse that marked her as a teacher of modest means but profound dedication.

Only now, after the passage of half a century, can I fully comprehend the mindset of that disheveled girl who had once been Miss Stephens' favorite student in third grade. The pursed lips, the uncombed hair, the expression that refused to conform to the expected norms of school photography—all these details speak to a young soul already carrying burdens too heavy for her years.

By the time that photograph was taken, at the end of third grade, Anjali was already enduring something that would scar her for decades to come.

CHAPTER 7
Jagdish, the Durga Devotee

The arrival of my brother Sandeep had shifted the entire dynamics of our household. Within weeks of his birth, the old servant woman whom I had always addressed as Mai was quietly dismissed, her services no longer deemed adequate for our family's evolving needs. In her place came Jagdish—a man who would assume not only all of Mai's former duties but expand his role far beyond what any of us initially imagined.

I remember Mai with a mixture of fondness and melancholy. Her long, bony fingers possessed a gentleness as she wielded a small wooden comb with closely set teeth, methodically coaxing lice from my long black hair in a ritual that was both practical and oddly comforting. She represented a kind of maternal constancy in my young life—someone who attended to the intimate, unglamorous necessities of childhood with unfailing care.

Before my brother's arrival, my straight hair had been my pride, falling in a dark curtain well below my shoulders. But a few months after my brother Sandeep's arrival, that same hair ended apologetically just above my ears—a stark, visible reminder that my mother's priorities had fundamentally shifted. She simply no longer possessed the energy or spare time to maintain the grooming rituals that had once been part of our daily routine, when without fail she would rub glycerin and rose water spiked with drops of fresh lemon juice to rub away the darkness from my complexion.

Like old Mai, Jagdish arrived at our doorstep without formal education—unable to read or write, uncertain even of his own birth year or month. These were common circumstances among the servant class, people whose lives were measured not by calendars and certificates but by the practical skills they could offer and the references that vouched for their character. He had come with a recommendation from another household, and in a neighborhood where news traveled faster than official announcements, everyone already knew about the birth of the long-awaited male child at 3B Bangla Sahib Lane and the family's urgent need to replace the old servant with someone more robust and capable.

Did my upwardly mobile parents consider this decision wise, given that their other two children were girls aged eight and five? In their minds, absolutely. They could hardly believe their good fortune in finding such a capable replacement so effortlessly, someone who appeared willing and able to work more hours for the same pay that Mai had received. The arrangement seemed perfect: where Mai had returned to her own home each evening, leaving the family to manage on their own, Jagdish would be a live-in presence. Suddenly, Susheila and Sohan Lal found themselves with unprecedented freedom—they could stay out as late as they wished, attend social functions without worrying about childcare, pursue their professional and social ambitions with newfound liberty.

The contrast between the old arrangements and the new was striking. Mai had been limited in her duties—she cooked simple meals and washed clothes, but little beyond that. Jagdish, however, seemed capable of everything: he would run errands throughout the city, massage my father's-tired legs after long days at the office, manage the household with an efficiency that impressed my parents immensely. It was, from their perspective, an unqualified improvement.

The other members of our domestic staff remained unchanged, creating a familiar backdrop against which Jagdish's presence stood out in sharp relief. There was still the same dark-skinned, curvaceous young cleaning woman who arrived five days a week to sweep and mop the concrete floors throughout our home and hand-wash the accumulated dirty kitchen wares that gathered in the corner by the water tap. The weathered gardener, his teeth stained red from years of chewing betel nut, continued his weekly visits to tend the foliage in our front lawn. And the shriveled woman with very dark skin—a member of the lowest caste whose presence was both essential and largely invisible—arrived every day without fail to clean the latrines at the very back of the courtyard and carry away our garbage, performing the tasks that no one else would touch.

When Jagdish first appeared at our doorstep, he presented a striking figure that would remain etched in my memory for decades. He was clad in a crisp white kurta pajama that spoke of careful preparation for this important moment, the fabric freshly laundered. In his hands, he clutched two items that would prove to define his presence in our home: a glass-framed picture of Ma Durga and a fan made of peacock feathers bound together with white cotton string. A ragged brown jute bag hung from his left shoulder, containing what I would later learn represented the entirety of his earthly possessions.

Jagdish was likely ten to fifteen years older than me, though his exact age remained as mysterious as his birth date. His personal history, pieced together from fragments of conversation and observation, painted a picture of profound hardship overcome through determination and skill. He had grown up in dire poverty in the foothills of the Himalayas, in the northernmost state of Jammu and Kashmir—a region that required a two-day train journey from Delhi, a distance that might as well have been another world for someone of his economic circumstances.

Like many people from that mountainous region, Jagdish possessed relatively light skin, a physical characteristic that carried complex social implications in a society where color often determined opportunity. Early in his life, driven by necessity and family obligation, he had become a skilled house servant, developing the versatile abilities that would eventually bring him to our door. His motivation was deeply personal: he sent most of his earnings home to support his widowed mother and a handicapped sister whose care fell entirely on his shoulders.

This dedication to family, combined with his apparent devotion to Ma Durga, provided exactly the kind of reassurance my parents craved. Here was someone who understood duty and devotion, whose character seemed grounded in the traditional values they respected. His religious commitment offered them a sense of security—surely someone so devoted to a Hindu goddess could be trusted with their children and their home.

It was in the summer of 1964, during one of those perfect early mornings that Delhi occasionally offers before the heat becomes unbearable, that I first encountered Jagdish in his new role. The temperature felt delightful against my bare arms, and the chirping of birds in our courtyard provided a soundtrack of natural harmony. My younger sister Sadhana and I were dressed in colorful cotton frocks with puffy short sleeves—outfits that reflected the progressive attitude of Lady Irwin School, which had abandoned dress codes when most other schools in Delhi maintained strict uniform requirements.

I was ready to walk to the bus stop with Sadhana trailing behind me, when my mother made an announcement that immediately struck me as odd: "This is Jagdish. He will escort you to the bus stop."

The strangeness of this arrangement wasn't lost on me. I had been walking to the bus stop unescorted with Sadhana for months, managing the responsibility with the pride that comes from being trusted with independence. Sadhana followed me everywhere despite my insistence on privacy, but that was a familiar annoyance, part of the natural order of sisterhood.

Jagdish looked down into my eyes with an expression I would later recognize as carefully calculated gentleness, speaking in a tone that was tender yet somehow practiced: "Baby, let me hold your bag and you hold your sister's hand."

I found myself staring at his face, taking in details that would become painfully familiar over the coming months. This was my first close encounter with a grown man sporting a handlebar mustache—the black whiskers curled upward with obvious care and pride. Most striking was a gold tooth on his upper left side that caught the morning light when he smiled, a detail that seemed both exotic and slightly menacing to my eight-year-old sensibilities. I nodded in reply.

This moment marked my first introduction to a worshipper of Durga—a devout Durga Bhagat whose faith would soon permeate every aspect of our household. Jagdish wasted no time in transforming our kitchen into what could only be described as a miniature temple dedicated to his chosen goddess. The wall facing the entry door was divided horizontally by three thick gray stone shelves that ran from end to end, originally installed to hold utensils and cooking necessities.

Under Jagdish's influence, the top shelf underwent a complete transformation, becoming the sacred sanctum for his glass-framed photograph of Durga. He established a daily ritual that never varied: each morning, before beginning any cooking duties, he would light a black incense blob positioned next to her picture. The incense would release a steady plume of aromatic smoke that curled upward toward the goddess's image, filling the kitchen with a scent that was both mystical and somehow oppressive.

My eight-year-old mind, already captivated by magic and mystery, proved fertile ground for Jagdish's teachings about Durga's immense powers. He possessed a storyteller's gift for making the divine seem immediate and accessible, describing Durga not as a distant deity but as an active force in the world. She was Mahamaya, he explained—the supreme shakti who had been personally summoned by the trinity of gods themselves. The three pillars of Hinduism—Shiva the transformer, Brahma the creator, and Krishna the preserver—had called upon her specifically to destroy evil wherever it might manifest.

The name "Durga," he taught me, came from "Durgatinashini," meaning "the slayer of enemies." She represented one of the most powerful manifestations of primal female energy, always depicted in imagery that conveyed both beauty and terrifying strength. In every representation, she sat regally upon a lion, draped in a red sari that symbolized power and passion, her right foot resting on her left thigh while her left toes-maintained contact with the ground.

Durga possessed intense, open eyes that seemed to see everything—the kind of gaze that could pierce through deception and reveal truth. Her mouth was closed in a slight smile that suggested both compassion and the knowledge of secrets beyond ordinary human understanding. A gold crown adorned her head, while golden ornaments decorated her neck, ears, and arms, each piece reflecting her divine status.

Her eight arms represented the eight cardinal directions, symbolizing her ability to protect devotees from threats approaching from any angle. Each handheld objects of specific significance: the lowest right hand was positioned in the Abhaya Mudra, the fear-relieving gesture that promised protection to faithful followers. Her other three right hands carried a trishul (a three-pronged spear for piercing illusion), a sword for cutting through ignorance, and a Sudarshan chakra (a flying disc that could pursue and destroy evil across any distance).

In her four left arms, beginning from the lowest, she held a lotus representing purity and spiritual awakening, a water pot symbolizing life-giving nourishment, a bow and arrow for focused intention and precise action, and a conch shell whose sound could awaken spiritual consciousness.

By praying to Durga, devotees can appease Rahu—the north node of the moon, considered a shadow planet in Vedic astrology. Wherever Rahu appears in an individual's birth chart, that area of life becomes a source of obsession and karmic challenge. Durga's intervention could help balance these influences, transforming destructive obsessions into productive spiritual energy.

Jagdish's devotion expressed itself through elaborate tantric rituals that he performed regularly, always with my sister and me as fascinated witnesses while our baby brother slept peacefully in his crib, oblivious to the spiritual theater unfolding around him. These ceremonies were unlike anything I had ever witnessed. Jagdish would twirl around in circles, chanting mantras in Sanskrit whose meanings remained mysterious but whose power seemed undeniable.

Throughout these rituals, he would wave his precious peacock feather fan with movements that seemed choreographed by some ancient knowledge. The fan itself was treated as a sacred object—Sadhana and I were strictly forbidden from touching it, as any contact from uninitiated hands would supposedly diminish its spiritual powers. The peacock feathers, with their iridescent eyes, seemed to watch us as Jagdish moved them through the air.

The practice of Tantra, as Jagdish explained it to our young minds, emphasized awakening the primordial feminine energy called Shakti within human beings. According to this tradition, Tantra viewed the human body not as something separate from the divine, but as a sacred dwelling place of all-knowing universal consciousness. Through proper ritual and devotion, practitioners could awaken dormant spiritual energies and achieve direct communication with divine forces.

Jagdish's influence extended beyond the spiritual realm into the most basic aspects of our daily life—our food. His cooking style differed dramatically from the simple, healing Ayurvedic fare that my grandmother had prepared during her visits. Where she had emphasized balance and digestive wellness through minimal spicing and traditional combinations, Jagdish created complex dishes that reflected his own temperament and moods.

He combined many more spices than we were accustomed to, creating flavor profiles that were intense and sometimes overwhelming. Copious amounts of onions and garlic appeared in his curries, ingredients that some traditional households avoided for their association with passion and agitation rather than spiritual calm. The flavor of our meals became a barometer of his emotional state—when he was pleased, the food sang with harmonious spices; when he was troubled or angry, the dishes carried an edge that made them difficult to enjoy.

Most significantly, Jagdish possessed an extraordinary ability to seduce my eight-year-old mind through a combination of magic tricks and Durga tales. I had never before encountered someone who possessed such extensive knowledge despite having never attended even primary school. His intelligence seemed to come from entirely different sources than the book learning I was receiving at Lady Irwin School—it was intuitive, mystical, and somehow more immediate and powerful than anything I encountered in classrooms.

The magic tricks he performed seemed to blur the line between entertainment and genuine supernatural ability. Simple sleight of hand became demonstrations of Durga's power working through her devoted servant. Stories of the goddess's battles against demons were told with such vivid detail that I could practically see the scenes unfolding before my eyes. Jagdish had a gift for making the mythological feel contemporary and personal, as if these ancient battles between good and evil were still being fought in the present moment, with consequences that could affect our own daily lives.

When the festival of Raksha Bandhan arrived on a full moon night in August 1964, it was celebrated with gusto in our household. On this day, a sister ties a sacred thread on her brother's wrist and then puts a sweet meat in his mouth. The brother takes a vow to protect his sister's honor and gives her a token gift of money. My little brother Sandeep was only three and a half months old, but my new adopted big brother Jagdish vowed to protect me from harm. From that day onwards I was instructed by my parents to not call him by his name but address him as "Bhaiya ji" or big brother.

Looking back now, I can see how carefully Jagdish cultivated my fascination and dependence.

CHAPTER 8
Offering to Durga

My father named me Anjali—a name that in Sanskrit means "an offering." The word carries the weight of devotion within it, referring to the sacred gesture performed with hands folded at the heart center, palms and fingers touching in supplication. Anjali mudra represents the soul's offering to the divine, a gesture of surrender and humility before forces greater than oneself.

I drew my first breath just before an angry summer sun prepared to set on May 14, 1956, entering the world at 7:03 PM in a hospital in New Delhi. According to the ancient science of Vedic astrology, the precise combination of planets and stars positioned in the sky at that exact moment painted a troubling picture for the newborn's future—tons of tears and strife were predicted to mark the path ahead. But my parents, Sohan Lal and Susheila, were focused on more immediate concerns: the delivery and room charges that represented a luxury they could barely afford, a financial strain that accompanied the joy of new life.

The circumstances of my birth carried their own weight within the complex expectations of Indian society. For their first child, most Indian parents pray fervently for a boy—a son who will carry forward the family name, perform the funeral rites for his parents, and bring honor rather than the financial burden traditionally associated with daughters. A girl with fair skin might be considered second best, a consolation prize that could at least promise a more favorable marriage arrangement. But I was a girl with dark skin and features inherited directly from my father's side.

Still, both my parents found reasons for gratitude. The child had arrived with ten toes and ten fingers—a blessing they didn't take for granted, especially considering it had taken two long years of trying for Susheila to conceive. In a culture where fertility is often seen as a reflection of divine favor, those years of waiting had carried their own burden of anxiety and social pressure.

My paternal grandmother, Gaura Devi, however, made no effort to hide her disappointment. She refrained from performing any of the traditional rituals that typically mark the joyous occasion of her oldest and most obedient son becoming a father. In her practical, unflinching assessment, this was hardly an occasion for celebration—the birth of a puny, dark-skinned girl whose eventual marriage would certainly demand a huge dowry.

By the time I reached my eighth year, our family constellation had expanded. I now had a five-year-old sister, Sadhana, who had been blessed with the fair skin and curly hair that mirrored our mother's appearance—features that would make her path through life notably smoother than my own. Most significantly, we had finally welcomed a newborn brother, Sandeep, whose arrival had been achieved only after two failed pregnancies that had taken a tremendous toll on Susheila's already frail constitution. Yet despite the physical cost, his birth was unquestionably worth every moment of suffering—a son at last, the answer to years of prayers and social pressure.

Our family's upward mobility had become increasingly evident in our living situation. We now resided in a sprawling bungalow in one of Delhi's most prestigious neighborhoods, situated directly across from a large park studded with a magnificent variety of deciduous trees. These elegant single-story brick houses along Bangla Sahib Lane had originally been constructed for British Civil Servants during the height of colonial power, and living in one represented a significant social achievement for an Indian family in the post-independence era.

CHAPTER 8

Sohan Lal's career had flourished beyond his earlier dreams. He now held the influential position of Director of Audio-Visual Education, commanding respect as the supervisor of over a hundred employees within the Ministry of Education in New Delhi. He had achieved what could only be described as his dream job—a position that required extensive socializing and offered opportunities to move within the circles of Delhi's educated elite.

For Susheila, her husband's professional success along with her own job as a medical social worker allowed her to be the queen of her household. Unlike her own mother and mother-in-law, who had lived their entire lives within the traditional confines of domestic duty, she was an educated woman who had transcended conventional limitations. She never needed to set foot in the kitchen for cooking duties, nor did she waste time performing the age-old religious rituals that had consumed so much of previous generations' energy. Her life was devoted to intellectual pursuits and social advancement rather than the mundane tasks of traditional housekeeping.

Sohan Lal threw himself into his work with passionate intensity, developing audiovisual aids that would revolutionize how Indian teenagers learned about their world. Both parents reveled in their demanding careers, which required frequent socializing, late-night functions, and networking events that were essential for professional advancement. They credited their domestic harmony to the hard work and dedication of Jagdish, who had begun treating Sohan Lal with the reverence and devotion of a son toward the father he had never known.

The kitchen had been completely transformed under Jagdish's influence, becoming the undisputed domain of both the servant and his beloved Durga Ma. The name "Jagdish" itself carries profound meaning in Sanskrit—"Lord of the world"—and he seemed determined to live up to that designation within the confines of our household.

My parents were genuinely impressed by the depth of his

religious knowledge and the sincerity of his devotion. They were particularly moved by his selfless financial sacrifice—sending most of his modest salary home to support his widowed mother and disabled sister, who struggled to maintain even a meager existence in the remote state of Jammu and Kashmir. This display of family loyalty resonated deeply with their own values, providing additional evidence of his fundamental decency and reliability.

The geographical connection held special significance as well. Durga Ma herself was believed to reside in that same mountainous region, dwelling within a sacred cave perched atop a formidable mountain peak that had become one of India's most famous and coveted pilgrimage destinations for devout Hindus. The fact that Jagdish hailed from the goddess's own homeland seemed to authenticate his spiritual credentials in my parents' eyes.

Within just two months of his arrival, Jagdish had accomplished something remarkable: he convinced my parents to embark on a pilgrimage to seek Durga's blessings while simultaneously meeting his mother and sister. The journey itself was an undertaking that demonstrated their growing trust in his judgment. The train journey to Jammu required two full days and one night of travel, carrying them through diverse landscapes as they moved from the plains of Delhi toward the foothills of the Himalayas.

At the base of the sacred mountain, they hired ponies for the steep climb to the cave temple, though many devoted pilgrims choose to walk barefoot up the treacherous mountain paths, considering this physical hardship an essential part of earning the privilege of Durga Ma's darshan. The entrance to the cave temple was narrow and cramped. One could only enter headfirst, like climbing into the mother's womb itself, an atmosphere of otherworldly mystery: ghee lamps flickered against wet stone walls that seemed to weep with ancient secrets, while the air grew thick with incense and the continuous chanting of Sanskrit mantras that had echoed in this sacred space for countless generations.

The pilgrimage proved to be a masterstroke in terms of solidifying Jagdish's position within our family. After witnessing his devotion in its natural habitat, after meeting his genuinely needy family members, after experiencing the profound spiritual atmosphere of Durga's mountain sanctuary, my parents' trust in him became complete. Any lingering doubts about his character or intentions were swept away by the powerful combination of religious authenticity and family obligation that the journey had revealed.

For eight-year-old me, this period marked the beginning of an intensive education in a form of spirituality unlike anything I had previously encountered. I had never before been in such intimate proximity to such a disciplined and knowledgeable Durga devotee. I would listen with rapt attention to his stories of the goddess and the magical powers she had supposedly bestowed upon him through his tantric practices. These weren't merely tales of ancient mythology—Jagdish presented them as contemporary reality, as ongoing relationships between himself and divine forces that continued to influence daily events.

Despite being completely illiterate, unable to sign his name with anything other than the imprint of his right thumb, Jagdish possessed a kind of intuitive wisdom that seemed to surpass formal education. Recognizing this limitation, he requested that I teach him how to write his name in Hindi script—a task that made me feel important and useful, creating an early bond between teacher and student that would prove crucial to his later manipulations.

My dependence on Jagdish grew gradually but steadily. He became my reliable source for tasty treats and carefully prepared school lunches that far exceeded anything my busy parents might have provided. Unlike my mother and father, who were frequently absent or distracted by their demanding careers and social obligations, Jagdish was always present and available. He possessed an almost supernatural ability to locate missing items —schoolbooks, pencils, watercolors, or any of the small but essential objects that seemed to vanish in the chaos of daily life. He attributed this talent to a special boon granted to him by Durga herself, and I had no reason to doubt his explanation.

With methodical patience, he began positioning himself as "the lord of my world," gradually assuming authority over my spiritual education by instructing me in the proper techniques for "pleasing Durga" so that I too might gain magical powers like his own. The lessons began innocuously enough, with simple daily rituals that seemed harmless and even spiritually enriching.

Each morning, I was required to offer one quarter of my favorite food to a faded colored depiction of Durga enclosed in a one-foot-square glass frame. This sacred image occupied a place of honor on the highest open black stone shelf in our kitchen, positioned above all the stainless steel and copper utensils in a location that emphasized its supreme importance within our domestic hierarchy.

According to Jagdish's detailed explanation of the process, Durga was supposed to emerge from her pictorial prison each afternoon to consume my offering in a display of divine favor. The system seemed to work with miraculous consistency: each day when I returned home from school, there was indeed nothing left in front of the picture, the food having been consumed by the goddess herself. This apparent miracle occurred just in time for me to witness Jagdish's elaborate evening prayer, during which he would grasp his precious peacock feather duster in his right hand and circle seven times on his right foot while mumbling mantras in a language I couldn't understand but whose power seemed undeniable.

The first crack in this carefully constructed illusion appeared on an ordinary day when I happened to notice a long trail of ants industriously devouring a quarter of a hard-boiled egg—my morning offering to the goddess. When I pointed this out to Jagdish, he said that Durga was upset and therefore had not personally partaken of the offering, leaving it vulnerable to lesser creatures.

When I pleaded with him to find out what had gone wrong, he agreed to intercede on my behalf by consulting directly with the goddess. He explained that Durga appeared to him when he entered deep meditative trances, providing specific instructions about how to proceed in various situations. After one such supposed consultation, he emerged with disturbing news: Devi had instructed him to begin teaching tantra to me. Only through this advanced spiritual practice, he claimed, would Durga agree to bestow the magical powers I so desperately wanted to possess. The whole learning process must be kept secret to ensure its potency.

It took only a couple of months for my eight-and-a-half-year-old mind to realize that tantra, as Jagdish practiced it, was not something I wanted to participate in. The specifics of what he demanded remain difficult to articulate even decades later, but my child's intuition screamed warnings that my rational mind was not yet equipped to process. When I began pleading with him to stop these "lessons," explaining that I no longer wanted to learn tantra or gain magical powers, Jagdish revealed an entirely different aspect of his personality.

My resistance was met with swift and calculated punishment designed to leave no visible evidence of abuse. If I refused to obey his instructions, he would first twist my wrists with precisely applied force, then move to twisting my thumb and middle fingers in ways that left me writhing in agony while producing no bruises that might alert outside observers. The pain was excruciating and the helplessness complete, but the torture was designed by someone who understood exactly how to inflict maximum suffering without creating physical evidence.

The psychological warfare proved even more devastating than the physical punishment. On days following my resistance, when I opened my lunch wrapped in old newspaper, the food would taste like chalk—a gritty, inedible substance that made clear his ability to control even my most basic needs. My beloved doll, patiently crafted with a bottle cap for a head and an empty Coke bottle for a body, would be found beheaded and violated, its small form mutilated in ways that seemed to promise worse consequences if I continued to disobey.

The most crushing aspect of this escalating abuse was my parents' complete inability to recognize what was happening under their own roof. Sohan Lal and Susheila remained absolutely convinced that Jagdish, being so obviously religious and hardworking, was simply not capable of traumatizing their daughter. In their eyes, I was a child who "always hid in dark corners with her head buried in a book"—a girl with such a vivid imagination that her complaints and stories could not be taken seriously.

The intellectual framework that my father brought to his assessment of my situation made my plight even more hopeless. Sohan Lal had studied Sigmund Freud extensively and was familiar with the psychoanalytic theory that children frequently fantasize about sexual abuse as a way of processing normal developmental anxieties. Armed with this sophisticated but misapplied knowledge, he dismissed my increasingly desperate pleas as textbook examples of childhood fantasy rather than cries for help from a daughter in genuine danger.

My mother, meanwhile, remained preoccupied with her own health concerns and the demands of maintaining her position within Delhi's competitive social circles. The combination of caring for a new baby, her frail constitution and managing her career left little energy for closely monitoring the emotional state of her older daughter, especially when the household seemed to be running so smoothly under Jagdish's capable management. Both parents had come to rely heavily on his services, not just for childcare but for maintaining their entire domestic infrastructure while they pursued their professional and social ambitions.

As my situation deteriorated, my parents began to view my crying and complaining as actively destructive forces that were "ruining the peace of their household." From their perspective, everything was functioning beautifully thanks to Jagdish's dedicated service, and my emotional outbursts represented an ungrateful attempt to disrupt this harmony. Many times, they would find me lying curled up on the cold concrete floor, sobbing and refusing to eat anything that Jagdish had prepared. Ultimately, however, hunger would always win these battles, forcing me to resort to what felt like further self-humiliation by consuming food prepared by my tormentor.

The isolation was perhaps the most devastating aspect of the entire ordeal. My younger sister Sadhana and baby brother Sandeep were far too young and innocent to grasp what was occurring around them. Even more bewildering was the silence of my grandmother, Gaura Devi, who resided with us intermittently and surely must have sensed that something was terribly wrong. Yet she never once spoke in my defense or questioned Jagdish's treatment of me.

Years later, I would understand that Gaura Devi's own vulnerability had compromised her ability to protect me. Her disabled right arm limited her physical capabilities, making her dependent on Jagdish's assistance for lifting and moving objects, as well as for running errands to local stores to replenish her stock of lentils, rice, vegetables, and other necessities. Significantly, she never ate Jagdish's cooking, instead preparing and consuming only food that she had made herself—a precaution that suggests she may have harbored her own suspicions about his character but felt powerless to act on them.

With no shoulder to cry on and no adult willing to validate my feelings of helplessness and terror, I was forced to shove these overwhelming emotions deep inside myself. The authority figures in my household had convinced me that I was crazy, that I was imagining everything, that my perceptions could not be trusted. This gaslighting proved as damaging as the abuse itself, teaching me to doubt my own reality and internalize the blame for my suffering.

My body began manifesting the trauma in ways that I couldn't understand or control. I resorted to self-soothing behaviors that focused obsessively on food and chewing, finding in these oral fixations some temporary relief from psychological pain that had no other outlet. By the end of my ninth year, I had gained significant weight and grown to become the tallest student in my fourth-grade class. The eating, however, brought its own complications as I added binge eating and purging to my daily routine, creating a cycle of consumption and rejection that mirrored my relationship with the household that was both nurturing and destroying me.

The physical symptoms multiplied and intensified as the months passed. My hands and feet began to sweat and swell profusely, making it difficult to walk normally or write with any comfort. A tight band seemed to form around my temples, creating a constant headache that was accompanied by a perpetually stuffy and swollen nose and eyes. Most tellingly, I began avoiding direct eye contact with others, keeping my gaze lowered and my hands clasped together whenever I was forced to interact with people outside our household.

Art became my salvation and my language for expressing what I could not say aloud. I formed an intense relationship with colors and shapes, using creative expression to distract my attention from the unresolved feelings of shame, guilt, and fear that threatened to overwhelm me. I doodled compulsively on every available surface—random pieces of paper, school textbooks, and even my own body, covering my thighs, legs, arms, and palms with intricate patterns that seemed to contain messages I couldn't consciously decode.

As I grew older, this artistic compulsion evolved into something bolder and more public. I began using acrylic paint to refresh my tired white sneakers, transforming them into unique canvases that added distinctiveness to my daily attire. These small acts of creative rebellion represented my attempt to maintain some sense of individual identity in a situation where every other aspect of my selfhood was under assault.

The outside world occasionally recognized my artistic abilities in ways that provided brief moments of validation amid the chaos. In fifth grade, I was selected along with twenty other children from all across India as winners of Shankar's International Art Contest—a tremendous honor that should have filled me with pride and confidence. Instead, my most vivid memory of the award ceremony involves standing in line to shake hands with the then-president of India, Dr. V.V. Giri, while being completely consumed with anxiety about my sweaty palms. I kept rubbing my hands together frantically, then wiping them on my clothes, utterly unable to focus on the significance of the moment. This memory of my physical discomfort drowns out everything else related to that achievement, a perfect example of how trauma had rewired my brain to prioritize survival concerns over normal childhood experiences of success and recognition.

School presented its own complicated landscape of choices and pressures that intersected with my home situation in complex ways. In sixth grade, students were offered a choice of credit-free classes in music, painting, or Sanskrit. The social dynamics surrounding these choices revealed the subtle hierarchies that governed our academic world: girls who selected Sanskrit were automatically labeled as nerds, students who were assumed to possess neither musical talent nor artistic sensibility. The implication was that Sanskrit represented a last resort for girls who lacked more appealing abilities. Now I wish I had studied Sanskrit as then I could easily understand the meaning of Sanskrit words that I encounter while studying various Vedic disciplines.

The most consequential academic decision arrived in ninth grade, when students were forced to choose their career trajectory: science or arts. This choice carried enormous social and economic implications in a society where science was aggressively sought after because it offered the clearest path to immigration opportunities. Scientists, engineers, and doctors were successfully relocating to America—which many Indians referred to as "Swarga Loka," or heaven on earth—creating a powerful incentive for academically capable students to pursue technical fields regardless of their natural interests or aptitudes.

I chose science to please my father, whose own professional success in educational innovation had made him a strong advocate for technical education. Yet even as I committed to this path, I found myself routinely studying the faces of girls who had chosen art over science, searching their expressions for clues about their emotional state. I envied them intensely and wondered about their family dynamics: didn't their parents want them to emigrate abroad? How had they gained the freedom to follow their passion?

CHAPTER 9
Father's Departure

Every morning at dawn, I would hear my father's measured breathing drift from the courtyard—deliberate inhales followed by holding his breath, then long controlled exhales that seemed to pull serenity from the very air. Sohan Lal practiced pranayama with the dedication of a man who understood that breath was life itself.

"Prana stands for life, and Yama means control," he would explain, his voice carrying the weight of ancient wisdom.

Each exhalation carried an almost imperceptible hum, a vibration that seemed to resonate with the rhythms of the cosmos. He believed that pranayama was more than a physical practice; it was an invitation to the soul to align with the eternal. During these early hours, the air in our courtyard felt charged with a sacred stillness, as though the universe paused to listen to his breath.

Five months before my eighteenth birthday, Sohan Lal's Prana Vayu—his life breath—was snatched away by Yama, the cosmic controller of life on earth. At forty-seven and in seemingly perfect health, my father's heart simply stopped. The clinical words on the death certificate were, "fatal heart attack".

The ancient texts tell us that Yama Dev controls the prana of all mortals, that each soul enters this world with a predetermined number of breaths. According to the Vedas, one's lifespan can be extended by slowing the rate of breathing. While humans breathe twelve to sixteen times per minute at rest, elephants draw only four breaths in that same span and can live up to

150 years when conditions support such longevity. Papa must have stretched his allotted time as far as his disciplined practice would allow, each morning's pranayama a gentle negotiation with mortality itself.

Sohan Lal was a devoted follower of Ma Kali, the fierce goddess of transformation and time. His spiritual guide was Shri Ramakrishna Paramahansa—the "premier swan," as the title translates—a 19th-century mystic who had achieved the rare state of divine realization. The small, uncrowded shrine dedicated to Kali stood a twenty- five-minute walk from our home, in the direction opposite to the popular Hanuman Temple where crowds gathered daily. In the evenings, Papa would walk barefoot alongside my mother Susheila, their feet connecting with the earth as they sought Ma Kali's blessings to transform and elevate their souls.

Unlike Jagdish, who performed daily rituals to please Durga, Sohan Lal's devotion to Ma Kali was simple and internal. No image of the dark goddess adorned our walls, but two glass-framed black-and-white photographs—each exactly one-foot square—held places of honor on the mantle above the unused fireplace in our children's bedroom. His guru's photograph claimed the right position, while the guru's wife, Ma Sarada Devi, gazed serenely from the left.

In his portrait, Shri Ramakrishna sits cross-legged upon the ground, clothed only in a simple white loincloth. His hair is cropped short, and a full beard frames his weathered face. What strikes the viewer most are his eyes—half-open, neither fully closed in meditation nor completely engaged with the physical world but suspended in that liminal space where the divine touches the mundane. His palms rest peacefully in his lap with fingers interlaced in the classic mudra of contemplation.

Beside him, Shri Sarada Devi mirrors his posture with feminine grace. White homespun cotton drapes her form, covering her torso, head, and bosom in the traditional manner of a Bengali woman. Her long, straight black hair frames a face that radiates both strength and compassion. Thick three-metal bracelets encircle each forearm. Both guru and Ma Sarada Devi had emerged from humble, rural origins; neither could read or write in the conventional sense, yet their illiteracy had never hindered their capacity to read the deepest truths of existence.

In the complex pantheon of Hindu deities, Kali represents one of the nine manifestations of Shakti, the divine feminine principle. Yet Papa, in his devotion, may have overlooked an important protocol: he should have first sought the blessings of Ganesh, Kali's mind-born son. This elephant-headed deity with a human torso serves as the gatekeeper to his mother's realm, the remover of obstacles on the spiritual path. Only through Ganesh's grace can human consciousness ascend from the base chakra where Shakti lies dormant, through the purification of all five energy centers, to unite with Shiva in the crown chakra at the top of the head.

In the sacred geography of the human body, Shakti resides coiled like a serpent at the base of the pelvis, in the muladhara chakra with four petals, guarded by her vigilant son. Meanwhile, Shiva's eternal abode rests at the crown of the head in the sahasrara —the thousand-petaled lotus chakra that blooms only when earthly consciousness merges with divine awareness.

My father's heart ceased its rhythm on the bone-chilling evening of December 31, 1974, just as the winter sun disappeared behind a veil of grey clouds. The irony was not lost on us: as the rest of the world prepared to celebrate the birth of a new year, our family faced the end of an era. Papa had been rushed to the hospital that morning, complaining of chest pains that would prove to be his final earthly suffering. By evening, his naked mortal remains returned to us in a black van, arriving just as our neighbors donned their sparkling attire for New Year's festivities.

His body was placed on the cold concrete floor of our living room, covered with a thin white cotton sheet that seemed insufficient protection against both the winter chill and the finality of death. The positioning—directly in front of our cold stone fireplace that had remained unused throughout all our years in that house—felt like a cruel irony. Relatives and friends, all draped in white as tradition demanded, gathered in our home. They squatted or sat cross-legged on cotton rugs, their bodies pressed shoulder-to-shoulder, creating a human barrier against the chilly breeze that entered through the wide-open front doors.

The silence that hung between sobs and wails was thick enough to cut with a knife, punctuated only by the occasional rustle of cotton clothing or the soft thud of someone shifting position on the hard floor. Darkness filled the room like grief itself. In what seemed like a collective failure of memory or custom, no one had thought to light a ghee lamp—that small flame that traditionally honors the departed soul during its forty-nine-day journey between worlds.

The morning after Papa's unexpected departure, his male relatives accompanied his body to the cremation grounds several miles beyond the city's edge. In accordance with tradition, the women stayed behind: my fourteen-year-old sister Sadhna, my forty-two-year-old mother Susheila, and I were enveloped by an overwhelming sense of sorrow that felt pervasive and stifling. Only my ten-year-old brother Sandeep was deemed old enough to witness the final ritual, his presence required as the family's future patriarch.

At the cremation ground, Papa's mortal remains were arranged with ceremonial care upon a pyre of seasoned wood. More logs were layered over his form, creating a wooden cocoon for his final transformation. As the pandit chanted Sanskrit mantras intended to guide his soul toward moksha—liberation from the cycle of birth and death—clarified butter was poured over the pyre. The ancient words rose like smoke into the winter air, invoking Agni, the fire god, to accept this offering and serve as messenger between the earthly and astral planes.

For nearly three hours, the voracious flames consumed what had once been my father, reducing decades of wisdom and love to ash and memory. In both marriages and deaths within Sanatan Dharma—the eternal law that governs righteous living—a havan or fire ceremony centers the ritual. The fire pit becomes the focal point where Sanskrit mantras capture the attention of various deities, creating a bridge between human supplication and divine response.

After the embers cooled to grey dust, tradition dictated that Sandeep, as the male heir, should gather the remaining ashes and bone fragments to carry them to the holy Ganges. There, the sacred waters would receive Papa's earthly remains and help his soul achieve final liberation. But Jagdish, our devoted big brother who had lived with us for nine years and helped raise Sandeep from infancy, stepped forward to perform this most formidable of duties.

Upon returning from the cremation grounds, Jagdish approached Sadhana and me with his characteristic tone of authority. "Papa ji was a saint," he announced, his voice carrying a mixture of awe and certainty. "In his skull, there was a hole at the top."

My eyes, already red-rimmed from hours of crying, widened at this revelation. I bit my lower lip to keep from crying out as my inner voice whispered with sudden understanding: *Your father Sohan Lal was indeed your hero. His soul must have departed through the highest gate.*

The flood of memories came unbidden: Papa's hands with their large palms and long fingers ending in perfectly square nails; his patient work refurbishing and painting furniture until each piece looked new again; his habit of reading books about the future of our planet, always seeking to understand humanity's destiny. Most clearly, I could hear his voice delivering his favorite piece of wisdom to us children: "They can steal everything from you—your possessions, your comfort, your security—but they cannot steal your education. Knowledge, once gained, becomes part of your very being."

My papa was the key figure in lighting a tiny flame of interest in Hatha Yoga and Sat karma (sacred duty). In early June when the summer vacations were in full swing, my father drove me to a newly opened Yoga Ashram. This Ashram belonged to Swami Direndra Brahamachari the yoga guru of the ruling prime minister of India Mrs. Indira Gandhi. Here yoga and body cleansing practices were taught free to the public. This was 1967 and yoga fever had not spread everywhere.

"Yes," I whispered to myself, the words barely audible above the wind rattling our windows, "my papa was my hero. His soul must be travelling to Satya Loka, the realm of pure truth. Meanwhile, I remain stuck here on the earth plane, though it feels more like Patal Loka—the underworld itself."

Ancient Vedic texts state that, at physical death, consciousness exits the body through one of nine gates: ears, eyes, nostrils, mouth, anus, or reproductive organ. These represent the portals through which we experience the material world during life.

But enlightenment is assured for the rare soul whose consciousness departs through the tenth gate, also known as Brahma Randhra—the crown of the head, where the sahasrara chakra blooms like a thousand-petaled lotus. This is the gateway reserved for those who have achieved spiritual realization, whose earthly journey has prepared them for direct union with the divine.

CHAPTER 10
Sukshma Sharira, Home of the Chakras

The ancient sages understood that existence operates on multiple levels simultaneously. According to Vedic wisdom, the vast cosmos contains fourteen distinct planes of existence, each vibrating at its own frequency of consciousness. We humans, bound by our physical senses and earthly concerns, remain familiar with only one: the Bhu Loka, our material realm of birth, growth, decay, and death.

Yet this earthly plane represents merely the middle ground in a vast spectrum of reality. Above our world stretch six higher planes of existence, realms of increasing subtlety and divine presence where enlightened beings dwell in states of consciousness we can barely imagine. Below us lie seven lower planes, domains where consciousness becomes increasingly dense, caught in the gravitational pull of base emotions and primitive desires.

But here lies the profound beauty of Vedic understanding: since the macrocosm finds perfect reflection in the microcosm, these same fourteen planes of existence manifest within each human being as subtle energy centers. These chakras, as Sanskrit tradition names them, transform our physical bodies into living temples, each one a universe complete within itself.

The Three Bodies: Vessels of Consciousness

The **Sthula Sharira**—our physical body—represents only the outermost layer of our being, the visible vehicle through which we interact with the material world. Dense and temporary, it serves as both temple and prison, allowing us to experience the pleasures and pains of earthly existence.

Within this physical shell resides the **Sukshma Sharira**, the subtle body that serves as home to all fourteen chakras. Papa had described this invisible form as an electrical blueprint of our physical being, a luminous template that shapes and sustains our material existence. In this subtle realm, thoughts take on tangible form, emotions generate real energy, and consciousness first encounters the patterns that will eventually manifest as physical experience. The fourteen chakras reside in this body.

At the deepest level dwells the **Karana Sharira**, the causal body that houses our eternal soul—that imperishable essence that carries forward from lifetime to lifetime, accumulating the fruits of our actions and the momentum of our desires. When death claims the physical form and even the subtle body eventually dissolves, this causal body continues its journey, seeking new forms through which to express its accumulated karma and fulfill its deepest aspirations.

The Sacred Geography Within

The journey begins with the **Muladhara chakra**, visualized as a four-petaled crimson lotus nestled at the perineum, where the physical body meets the earth's energy. Here, coiled like a sleeping serpent, rests Kundalini Shakti—the primordial feminine power that, when awakened, can transform human consciousness into divine awareness. But before this foundational chakra can function properly, seven lower centers must first be purified and balanced. These **animal chakras**, extending from the pelvis down to the soles of the feet, represent the primitive aspects of consciousness that keep us bound to survival-based thinking and reactionary emotions.

Reading their names felt like encountering old enemies I had never consciously recognized:

Atala—the realm of fear, where consciousness contracts in anticipation of threats both real and imagined. I recognized this energy in the way my body had seized with terror when we received news of Papa's heart attack.

Vitala—the domain of anger, where frustrated desires burst into flames of rage and resentment. How many times had I felt this fire burning in my chest when life failed to meet my expectations?

Sutala—the breeding ground of jealousy, where comparison becomes poison and others' happiness feels like personal loss. Even now, I caught myself envying friends whose fathers still lived.

Talatala—the fog of confusion, where clear thinking dissolves into mental chaos and decision-making becomes impossible. This had been my state for days, unable to think beyond the immediate shock of loss.

Rasatala—the fortress of selfishness, where every action revolves around personal gain and the world shrinks to the size of one's own desires. I winced, recognizing how often my spiritual seeking had been motivated by what I could gain rather than how I could serve.

Mahatala—the darkness of inner blindness, where wisdom cannot penetrate and truth remains hidden behind layers of self-deception. How much of my life had I spent stumbling in this darkness, mistaking shadows for reality?

Patala—the deepest pit of hatred, where love cannot take root and every encounter becomes an opportunity for violence, whether physical, emotional, or spiritual.

The Ascending Path of Transformation

When an individual commits to eliminating these seven poisons —hatred, inner blindness, selfishness, confusion, jealousy, anger, and fear— something miraculous occurs. The Muladhara chakra, no longer dragged downward by the gravitational pull of base emotions, begins to stabilize and function according to its true purpose: creating an unshakeable foundation of safety and security that comes not from external circumstances but from deep trust in the cosmic order.

This stabilization creates the conditions for consciousness to rise to the **Swadhisthana chakra**, depicted as a six-petaled lotus located just below the navel. Here, ego develops in its healthy form—not as the destructive pride that separates us from others, but as the necessary sense of individual identity that allows us to function effectively in the world while maintaining awareness of our connection to the whole.

From here, energy naturally progresses to the **Manipura chakra** at the solar plexus, visualized as a ten-petaled lotus blazing with the fire of personal power. This solar chakra serves as a crucial transformer, taking the raw energy of the lower centers and refining it into the subtle power needed to access the heart. Connected to both the subconscious mind and the physical digestive system, it increases willpower and inner drive when properly awakened.

The Heart's Opening and Beyond

Only when the Manipura achieves complete stability can consciousness make the quantum leap to the **Anahata chakra** —the twelve-petaled lotus of the heart center where universal love and compassion naturally arise. This is not the emotional love that depends on conditions and preferences, but the unconditional acceptance that recognizes the divine presence in all beings.

The journey continues upward to the **Vishuddhi chakra** at the throat, depicted as a sixteen-petaled lotus where communication transcends mere exchange of information to become an expression of divine truth. Here, words carry the power to heal or harm, to reveal or conceal, to liberate or enslave.

At the eyebrow center sits the **Ajna chakra**, the famous third eye visualized as a two-petaled lotus. When this center opens through dedicated practice and grace, it gifts the individual with direct perception of universal consciousness—the ability to see beyond the veil of appearances into the underlying unity that connects all existence.

Finally, at the crown of the head, lies the ultimate destination: the **Sahasrara chakra**, the thousand-petaled lotus. Here individual consciousness merges with cosmic consciousness. When awareness reaches this exalted state, the person becomes enlightened like a Buddha, attaining moksha—that liberation characterized by nirvana and everlasting contentment.

The hole that Jagdish had discovered at the top of Papa's skull suddenly took on profound significance. This physical opening represented the completion of a spiritual journey that had taken years of dedicated practice, a sign that consciousness had successfully navigated the entire spectrum of human potential and graduated beyond the need for earthly experience.

The Five Elements: Gateways to Transformation

The five elements of creation—earth, water, fire, air, and ether—each reside within specific energy centers and govern our capacity to experience the world through our five senses.

The **earth element** in the Muladhara chakra governs our sense of **smell**, that most primitive and survival-oriented of senses that can instantly transport us to memories and emotions. By refining our relationship with scent—learning to appreciate natural fragrances while avoiding synthetic stimulation—we begin to purify the foundation chakra.

The **water element** in the Swadhisthana chakra governs **taste**, our relationship with pleasure and desire. By choosing foods that support clarity and avoiding those that cloud awareness, we gradually purify the creative center.

The **fire element** in the Manipura chakra governs **sight**, perhaps our most dominant sense in the modern world. The practice of "soft gazing"—looking at the world with relaxed attention rather than the aggressive staring that exhausts the nervous system—allows us to develop conscious seeing. Through conscious seeing, we develop the inner fire that transforms experience into wisdom.

The **air element** in the Anahata chakra governs **touch**, our capacity for physical and emotional intimacy. Human hands demonstrate the power of conscious touch that heals.

The **ether (akasha) element** in the Vishuddhi chakra governs **sound**, the vibration that creates and destroys worlds.

By training and refining these five senses through conscious practice, the corresponding chakras purify themselves, eventually granting access to the sixth sense—that intuitive perception that transcends physical limitations and opens direct communication with universal consciousness.

CHAPTER 11
Ganesha, Lord of the Five Sense Organs

In the pristine heights of the Himalayas, where snow-capped peaks touch the heavens and ancient caves hold the secrets of creation, Devi Parvati had created a sacred sanctuary. This was no ordinary bathing place, but a divine pool carved, fed by waters that had never known earthly pollution. The cave itself pulsed with primordial energy; its walls embedded with gems that caught and reflected the cosmic light.

Thousands of years ago, on the fourth day of the waxing moon in the Vedic month of Magha (February), during the sandhi period in early morning when darkness leaves and daylight comes, Devi Parvati prepared for her bath. Her husband Shiva had already ventured into the forest on the back of Nandi, his white bull, to gather sacred herbs.

The timing was crucial—the fourth day of the waxing moon represents the building of positive energy, while Magha is the month when spiritual practices bear the most fruit. Finding herself alone, Shakti gathered the golden-hued dead skin that naturally flaked from her divine form—each particle containing the essence of creation itself. With her hands, she lovingly shaped this sacred material into the form of a perfect child. Then, channeling the life force that flows through all existence, she breathed her divine consciousness into the form. The child's eyes opened with the wisdom of ages, and she named him Ganesha, meaning "Lord of the Ganas" (divine attendants).

"My beloved son," Parvati said, her voice carrying the music of creation, "guard this entrance while I take my bath. Allow no one to enter."

Ganesha, though newly born, possessed an ancient soul and understood the gravity of his task. He took his position at the cave entrance with the dignity of a seasoned guardian.

While Parvati was immersed in her sacred waters, chanting mantras that harmonized with the cosmic vibrations, Shiva returned earlier than expected. Arriving on Nandi, he approached the familiar cave with the casual confidence of one entering his own home.

Ganesha stepped forward, his small but determined form blocking the entrance. "Stop! You are not permitted to enter. My mother is taking her bath."

Shiva, whose third eye had witnessed the birth and destruction of countless universes, was taken aback. His famous temper, which had once reduced the god of love to ash, began to flare. "Who are you, child, to deny me entry to my own dwelling? I know of no son born to us!"

"I am Ganesha, son of Parvati, and I follow her commands above all else," the boy replied with unwavering resolve.

The confrontation escalated as neither would yield. Shiva's cosmic pride clashed with Ganesha's absolute devotion to his mother's wishes. In a moment of divine fury that shook the mountains, Shiva raised his trident—the weapon that maintains cosmic balance—and severed Ganesha's head from his body.

The sound echoed through dimensions, and Shakti, sensing the disturbance in the cosmic order, rushed from her sacred pool.

"Mahadeva!" she cried, her voice carrying both love and reproach. "How could you destroy the child I created with my own essence? He was only following my instructions! Restore his life immediately or face the consequences of a mother's wrath!"

Shiva, seeing his beloved's pain and recognizing his error, immediately set about rectifying his action. However, the original head was too damaged by the cosmic force of his trident. Looking around desperately, his gaze fell upon a baby elephant.

With reverent care, Shiva placed the elephant's wise head upon Ganesha's human torso, channeling the life force back into the body. As consciousness returned, Ganesha opened his eyes—now the kind, intelligent eyes of an elephant—and smiled at both his parents.

The Significance of the Elephant Head

This transformation was no accident but divine wisdom manifesting. The elephant possesses the most sophisticated sensory apparatus in the animal kingdom. Its trunk contains over 40,000 muscles and serves as hand, nose, and communication device all in one. Elephants never forget, symbolizing the retention of spiritual wisdom. They can hear infrasonic communications across vast distances, representing the ability to perceive subtle spiritual vibrations. Their gentle nature despite immense strength embodies the ideal of power controlled by wisdom.

The Contest Between Brothers

Time passed, and Shiva, desiring a child born of his own essence, created Kartikeya from his divine seed. Where Ganesha embodied earthy wisdom and accessibility, Kartikeya radiated solar brilliance and martial prowess. Kartikeya chose the magnificent peacock as his vehicle—a bird that soars high and displays cosmic beauty. Ganesha, showing his characteristic humility and wisdom, preferred a small brown mouse named Mooshak as his companion.

The mouse choice puzzled many, but Ganesha understood its profound symbolism. Mice can penetrate the smallest spaces, representing the ability to overcome any obstacle. They are also notorious for nibbling through things, symbolizing the gradual destruction of ego and ignorance.

As the universe expanded under Shiva and Shakti's creative force, prayers from countless beings flooded the cosmic realm. Humans, animals, plants, and even celestial beings sought divine intervention to remove obstacles from their spiritual paths. The cosmic parents realized they needed to designate one of their sons as the primary remover of obstacles for those seeking to master their five senses and achieve liberation.

A contest was declared. Both sons were to circumambulate the entire universe three times, and whoever completed this task first would earn the coveted title.

Kartikeya, confident in his peacock's speed and his own martial prowess, immediately mounted his radiant vehicle. With a flash of brilliant feathers and cosmic fire, he soared into the vastness of space.

All the assembled gods, goddesses, and celestial beings looked at Ganesha sitting cross-legged before his parents. The pot-bellied deity stood slowly, his movements deliberate and thoughtful. He lifted his trunk in salutation, approached his tiny mouse with great dignity, and carefully mounted the patient creature.

Then, in a moment that would echo through eternity as the perfect example of spiritual understanding, Ganesha guided Mooshak (mouse) in three slow, reverent circles around Shiva and Shakti. With each circumambulation, he chanted the Gayatri mantra honoring the source of all creation. Finally, he dismounted and seated himself in perfect lotus position before his parents.

The cosmic assembly waited in puzzled silence until Shiva, raising his left eyebrow in the gesture that precedes divine inquiry, asked, "Beloved son, the contest was to circle the universe three times. How do you claim to have completed this task?"

Ganesha's response resonated with the wisdom of ages: "Revered Father, beloved Mother, you are the universe. All creation springs from your union, exists within your consciousness, and ultimately returns to your divine essence. To circle you with devotion and understanding is to encompass all existence. I have indeed traveled the universe three times."

A profound silence fell over the assembly as the depth of this truth settled into every consciousness present. Shakti's face illuminated with pride and joy. She clapped her hands, and the sound created new stars. "My brilliant son, you have pierced the veil of maya (illusion) and perceived the ultimate reality. You understand that the macrocosm exists within the microcosm, that the infinite dwells within the heart of every seeker. You are truly worthy to guide beings toward mastery of their senses and removal of all obstacles."

The gathering erupted in celebration. "Ganesh ki jai ho! Victory to Ganesha!" echoed through all dimensions.

Divine Rewards and Sacred Marriage

The gods and goddesses honored Ganesha with celestial feasts where amrita (divine nectar) flowed freely, and the music of the Gandharvas or celestial angels provided entertainment. In recognition of his wisdom and new role, he was offered the hands of Riddhi and Siddhi, the two daughters of Lord Brahma.

Riddhi, whose name means "abundance," embodied all forms of prosperity—material, spiritual, emotional, and intellectual. She ensures that Ganesha's devotees never lack what they truly need for their spiritual evolution.

Siddhi, representing "spiritual powers" or "accomplishments," grants the supernatural abilities that naturally arise when the senses are fully mastered. These include telepathy, clairvoyance, the ability to heal, and other psychic gifts that serve spiritual evolution.

It is taught that sincere devotees of Ganesha receive both these blessings: the abundance necessary for spiritual practice and the paranormal insights that arise from purified consciousness.

Guardian of the Muladhara Chakra

From that cosmic moment forward, Ganesha assumed his role as the divine gatekeeper to Parvati's sacred dwelling within the human body. This cave exists in the Muladhara chakra, located at the perineum in males and at the cervical opening in females. Here, the primordial Shakti energy lies dormant as Kundalini, awaiting awakening through spiritual practice.

The Sacred Iconography

Every aspect of Ganesha's appearance carries profound spiritual meaning:

The Elephant Head represents the developed intellect that has transcended ordinary human limitations. Elephants symbolize:

- **Memory**: The ability to retain spiritual teachings and experiences
- **Wisdom**: Deep understanding that comes from integrating knowledge with experience
- **Gentleness**: Power tempered with compassion
- **Obstacle Removal**: The elephant's ability to clear paths through the densest jungle

The Pot Belly symbolizes the capacity to digest all experiences—pleasant and unpleasant—transforming them into wisdom. It represents:

- **Acceptance**: Embracing all of life without resistance
- **Transformation**: Converting challenges into growth opportunities
- **Contentment**: The satisfaction that comes from inner fullness

The Four Hands represent mastery over the four directions of consciousness and the four goals of human life (dharma, artha, kama, moksha). Each hand carries specific symbolism:

- **Upper Right Hand (Goad)**: The tool for prodding the mind toward truth, representing discrimination

between real and unreal
- **Upper Left Hand (Conch Shell)**: The primordial sound (AUM) from which creation emerges, representing the power of sacred sound
- **Lower Left Hand (Laddu/Modak)**: The sweet reward of spiritual practice, representing the joy found in divine connection
- **Lower Right Hand (Blessing Mudra)**: The gesture of fearlessness and boon-granting, offering protection and spiritual gifts

The Red Cobra coiled around his waist represents:
- **Mastery over Time**: The serpent symbolizes cyclical time, which the enlightened being transcends

The Kundalini Connection

At the base of every human spine, in the subtle body (sukshma sharira), lies the dormant cosmic energy called Kundalini—depicted as a coiled black serpent with three and a half coils. This represents the unmanifested creative power that, when awakened, rises through the chakras, transforming consciousness at each level.

Ganesha guards this tremendous force because premature awakening without proper preparation can be dangerous. The five senses must first be purified and controlled. The practitioner must develop:
- **Ethical behavior (Yamas and Niyamas)**
- **Physical health through yoga**
- **Breath control through pranayama**
- **Mental concentration through meditation**
- **Devotion through bhakti practices**

Only when these foundations are solid does Ganesha grant permission for the Kundalini to safely rise, blessing the practitioner with progressive spiritual unfoldment.

Planetary Correspondence

Ganesha's worship strengthens Mercury (Budha) in one's astrological chart. Mercury governs:

- **Communication**: Clear, truthful expression
- **Intelligence**: Practical wisdom and learning ability
- **Manifestation**: The power to bring ideas into reality
- **Discrimination**: The ability to distinguish truth from falsehood

As "Budha" (the wise one), Mercury represents the enlightened intellect that serves spiritual evolution rather than mere worldly success.

CHAPTER 12
Shiva, the First Yogi

In the pristine silence of the highest Himalayas, sits the eternal figure who embodies the very essence of yoga itself. Shiva, in his meditative form, represents the Adi Yogi—the first and ultimate practitioner of yoga.

Mount Kailash rises behind him like a dark grey pyramid piercing the sky, its peak forever unconquered by human feet. This is no ordinary mountain but the mythical Mount Meru—the cosmic axis that connects earthly consciousness to the astral realms, like the spinal column in a human body.

Lake Mansarovar, known as the "Lake of the Mind," spreads before him like a mirror reflecting infinite consciousness. It is the highest freshwater lake on Earth. The luminous crescent moon adorning Shiva's left temple represents the cooling, receptive aspect of consciousness that balances the solar fire of spiritual awakening, while the clear blue sky above speaks of limitless awareness.

Shiva sits upon a tiger skin, representing his mastery over the most primal and dangerous aspects of nature. The tiger symbolizes the untamed mind, raw passion, and the fierce ego that must be conquered before true spiritual progress can begin. By sitting upon this skin, Shiva demonstrates that he has not destroyed these forces but transformed them.

Every inch of Shiva's powerful form is covered with sacred ash, transforming his living flesh into the appearance of a statue carved from stone. Ash represents what remains after fire has consumed all that is destructible, symbolizing the eternal essence that survives physical dissolution. Covering oneself with ash represents the ego's dissolution in the face of cosmic truth.

Coiled around Shiva's neck three and a half times is the great serpent Vasuki. The serpent's three and a half coils mirror the dormant spiritual energy that lies coiled at the base of the human spine. Serpents symbolize cyclical time. Snakes shed their skin, representing the continuous renewal of consciousness.

Though closed in meditation, Shiva's third eye—located between his eyebrows—represents the inner vision that perceives truth directly. When opened, this eye has the power to reduce illusion to ash through the fire of pure knowledge.

Shiva's subtle smile reveals the deep contentment that arises from perfect self-realization. This is not the happiness that depends on external circumstances but the inherent bliss of consciousness recognizing its own infinite nature.

Shiva demonstrates the ideal meditation posture, the lotus pose, with legs folded and feet resting on opposite thighs. This position creates a closed circuit that prevents spiritual energy from dissipating and balances the body weight evenly while maintaining spinal alignment.

His hands rest on his knees in Gyan mudra, where the tip of the thumb touches the tip of the index finger, forming a circle while the three other fingers remain straight. A necklace of 108 Rudraksha beads hangs around his neck, each the size of a large cherry. These beads are formed from Shiva's tears of compassion for humanity's suffering.

Standing in the earth beside him is a Trishul. The three-pronged weapon represents the three attributes of nature or Tri Gunas: Sattva (purity), rajas (activity), and tamas (inertia)—the fundamental forces that govern all manifest existence.

Golden rays pour forth from Shiva's heart center, revealing the Anahata chakra in its fully awakened state. This luminous sun within the chest represents the heart chakra opened to its fullest capacity, radiating universal compassion.

Despite his ascetic practices, Shiva displays a powerful, well-proportioned physique—muscular arms, broad chest, and defined abdominal muscles. This teaches that true spirituality enhances rather than diminishes physical vitality.

From the perspective of spiritual astrology, Shiva's worship particularly strengthens Surya (the Sun) in one's birth chart. The Sun represents:

Creative Potential: The fundamental life force that drives all growth and evolution toward enlightenment. When strong, it grants:

- **Leadership Abilities**: Natural authority based on wisdom rather than force
- **Creative Expression**: The power to manifest one's spiritual insights in the world

Father Principle: The Sun also represents the father archetype—the protective, guiding force that provides structure and discipline. Shiva worship helps heal:

- **Father Wounds**: Difficulties in relationships with authority figures
- **Self-Authority**: The ability to become one's own wise guide
- **Protective Instincts**: Developing healthy boundaries and discernment
- **Mentorship**: The capacity to guide others on their spiritual path

Shiva is traditionally associated with cannabis (ganja), which still grows wild along the sacred Ganges River. In ancient texts, cannabis is called "Vijaya" (victory), indicating its role in achieving victory over mental limitations.

Ayurvedic medicine classifies the marijuana plant as:

- **Fire Element Enhancer**: Increasing metabolic and

digestive fire (agni)
- **Consciousness Expander**: Opening new pathways of perception
- **Stress Reliever**: Calming the nervous system for deeper meditation
- **Sacred Sacrament**: A tool for religious and spiritual practices when used mindfully

Dr. Raphael Mechoulam's groundbreaking 1992 discovery of anandamide—the "bliss molecule"—revealed that the human body naturally produces compounds like cannabis:

The Endocannabinoid System: This biological network in the human body helps regulate:

- **Mood and Emotion**: Natural mechanisms for achieving emotional balance
- **Pain and Inflammation**: The body's innate healing responses
- **Memory and Learning**: How consciousness processes and integrates experiences
- **Appetite and Sleep**: Basic functions that support overall well-being

Therapeutic Applications:

- **Reduce Anxiety**: Calming an overactive nervous system
- **Enhance Neuroplasticity**: Creating new neural pathways for healing
- **Deepen Meditation**: Facilitating states of inner stillness and concentration
- **Process Emotions**: Allowing suppressed feelings to surface and be released

CHAPTER 13

Krishna, the Diplomat

The Moon, Earth's closest celestial companion, completes its orbital dance around our planet every 29 days, creating the rhythmic cycles that have guided human consciousness since time immemorial. Ancient Vedic sages, through millennia of observation and inner exploration, recognized the Moon as the primary influence on human emotions and mental states.

Just as the Moon's gravitational pull governs the ocean's tides, it similarly affects the water within our bodies—which comprises approximately 72% of our physical form. This water carries our emotional essence, and its fluctuations mirror the lunar phases with remarkable precision. The ancient yogis understood that emotions are not random occurrences but follow predictable patterns linked to cosmic rhythms.

The Lunar Phases and Consciousness:

Shukla Paksha (Waxing Phase): During the bright fortnight, as the Moon grows from new to full, human emotions tend toward expansion, optimism, and outward expression. This is the time of increasing energy, new beginnings, and manifestation of desires.

Krishna Paksha (Waning Phase): During the dark fortnight, as the Moon diminishes from full to new, consciousness naturally turns inward. This period favors introspection, release of old patterns, and spiritual contemplation.

This understanding forms the foundation of the Vedic calendar, where all festivals and spiritual observances are timed according to lunar phases to maximize their psychological and spiritual impact.

Lord Krishna emerges from this lunar understanding as the deity who governs and harmonizes emotional life. Krishna specifically guides the transformation of human emotion from attachment to pure love and devotion. The moon in an individual's birth chart gets "happy" upon Krishna worship.

Krishna's deep blue-black skin color—his darkness contains all possibilities. The Peacock Feather Crown represents true nobility that comes from inner divine nature. Perhaps Krishna's most iconic attribute, the bamboo flute represents the irresistible call of the divine that draws all souls homeward. His silk robes and gold jewelry show us the path of integration, the path that transforms rather than abandons worldly life.

The striking differences between Krishna and Shiva represent complementary approaches to spiritual realization:

Shiva - The Path of Renunciation:

- **Appearance**: Ash-covered body symbolizing transcendence of worldly attachments
- **Habitat**: Mountain peaks and cremation grounds, representing withdrawal from society
- **Practice**: Deep meditation and cosmic dance, emphasizing inner transformation
- **Ornaments**: Simple Rudraksha beads and the serpent Vasuki, representing mastery over time and death
- **Relationship**: Devoted to one consort, Parvati, symbolizing the union of consciousness and energy

Krishna - The Path of Engagement:

- **Appearance**: Dark complexion representing the infinite depth of divine mystery, adorned in fine silk

and gold
- **Habitat**: Vrindavan's lush forests and the banks of the Yamuna River, representing engagement with life's beauty
- **Practice**: Music, dance, and divine play (lila), emphasizing joy and celebration
- **Ornaments**: Peacock feather crown and bamboo flute, representing natural beauty and divine music
- **Relationships**: Multiple marriages and the legendary love with Radha, symbolizing the soul's many relationships with the divine

Krishna in the Mahabharata

The Kurukshetra War represents the eternal battle between dharma (righteousness) and adharma (unrighteousness) that occurs both in the world and within every human heart.

The Pandavas' loss of their kingdom through gambling represents how souls become entangled in maya (illusion) through attachment and poor choices. Their subsequent exile symbolizes the purification process necessary before spiritual victory.

The Bhagavad Gita: Timeless Wisdom for Modern Challenges

Krishna's discourse to Arjuna on the battlefield remains one of humanity's greatest spiritual treasures, addressing universal questions that plague every generation:

The Setting's Significance: A battlefield represents:

- **Life's Conflicts**: Every day presents choices between higher and lower impulses
- **Moral Ambiguity**: Rarely are ethical decisions black and white

- **Crisis Points**: Moments when superficial solutions fail and deeper wisdom becomes necessary
- **Transformation Opportunities**: Conflicts that force spiritual growth

Arjuna's Dilemma: His paralysis before battle represents:
- **Compassion Confusion**: When kindness seems to conflict with necessary action
- **Role Uncertainty**: Struggling to understand one's purpose in life
- **Emotional Overwhelm**: When feelings threaten to paralyze appropriate response
- **Spiritual Crisis**: The dark night of the soul that precedes enlightenment

Krishna's Teaching Methods:
- **Multiple Perspectives**: Presenting various yogic paths to suit different temperaments
- **Practical Wisdom**: Connecting philosophical principles to immediate decisions
- **Compassionate Guidance**: Understanding human limitations while pointing toward transcendence
- **Divine Authority**: Speaking from the perspective of ultimate truth

CHAPTER 14
SwarBhanu, the Clever Dragon

The vast tapestry of Vedic literature weaves intricate stories of cosmic forces personified as divine beings—Devas (luminous gods) and Asuras (shadow beings). Among these tales, none is more psychologically revealing than the story of SwarBhanu, the clever dragon whose audacious theft of immortality forever changed the cosmic order.

When I first examined my Vedic birth chart (Janam Kundali) and discovered the placement of the two shadow planets—Rahu (the dragon's head) and Ketu (the headless body)—a chill of recognition ran through my being. There, in stark mathematical precision, lay the cosmic signature of my soul's journey.

The inner voice whispered with unmistakable clarity: "In your chart, the dragon's head sits in the first house alongside Saturn—a dreaded combination known as Shrapit Yoga, the 'cursed union.'"

The implications hit like a thunderbolt. What karmic debts from countless past lives had I accumulated to deserve the two most challenging planetary influences occupying the same house—the very house that governs conscious identity and ego development?

Yet as fear gave way to deeper understanding, I began to glimpse the profound spiritual opportunity hidden within this apparent cosmic curse. For Rahu and Ketu, when reunited in consciousness, form the complete being of SwarBhanu, which means the "splendor of radiance."

The story of Rahu and Ketu emerges from one of Vedic

literature's most symbolic narratives—the Sagar Manthan, or "churning the ocean of consciousness."

The Devas (positive forces) found themselves weakened and unable to obtain Amrit—the nectar of immortality that represents enlightened consciousness. Recognizing their limitation, they made a strategic alliance with their traditional enemies, the Asuras (shadow forces).

Lord Vishnu, the preserver god, took the form of Kurma (the cosmic tortoise), providing an unshakeable foundation for the churning process. The tortoise, with its ability to withdraw into its shell, represents the capacity for introversion necessary for deep inner work.

Mount Meru, symbolizing the human spinal column, served as the churning rod. In spiritual anatomy, Sushumna the central channel through which consciousness ascends from material to divine awareness is present inside the spinal column connecting the seven higher chakras.

The serpent Vasuki served as the churning rope. He has five heads, representing the five senses. The Devas grasped Vasuki's tail while the Asuras pulled his heads. As the churning intensified, a deadly blue poison (Halahala) emerged first representing the toxins that surface when we begin deep psychological work. Past traumas, suppressed emotions, and negative patterns must be faced before hidden talents can be accessed. When the poison threatened to destroy all creation, Lord Shiva consumed it, holding it in his throat rather than swallowing it. His throat turned blue, earning him the name "Neelkanth" (blue-throated one). This teaches that advanced consciousness can neutralize negativity by neither rejecting it nor being overwhelmed by it but holding it in awareness until it transforms.

The fourteen precious objects emerged from the ocean depths:
1. **Halahala** (the poison) - Representing purification through facing difficulties

2. **Kaustubha** (the divine gem) - Spiritual insight and discrimination
3. **Parijata** (the celestial tree) - Wish-fulfillment through aligned will
4. **Varuni** (the goddess of wine) - Divine intoxication and transcendence
5. **Dhanvantari** (the divine physician) - Healing and wholeness
6. **Lakshmi** (the goddess of abundance) - Prosperity in all forms
7. **Rambha** (the celestial nymph) - Beauty and artistic inspiration
8. **Ratnas** (precious gems) - Various spiritual attainments
9. **Kamadhenu** (the wish-fulfilling cow) - Abundance and nourishment
10. **Airavata** (the white elephant) - Royal power and dignity
11. **Apsaras** (celestial dancers) - Joy and celebration
12. **Shankha** (the conch shell) - Sacred sound and communication
13. **Gada** (the mace) - Spiritual strength and protection
14. **Amrit** (the nectar of immortality) - Ultimate realization and deathlessness

At the end, when the Amrit rose to the surface, Lord Vishnu transformed into Mohini, the enchanting goddess, to distribute the nectar exclusively to the Devas. Nearly all the Asuras fell under her spell. SwarBhanu alone saw through the illusion. Disguising himself among the Devas, he boldly seated himself between the Sun and Moon—the two luminaries who represent the conscious mind and emotional make up of a human being.

As SwarBhanu raised the nectar to his lips, the Sun and Moon recognized his true nature and alerted Vishnu. But it was too late

—the nectar had touched his throat. Through pure audacity and intelligence, a being had transcended his ordained nature.

Vishnu, realizing his mistake, sent the Sudarshan Chakra present on his right little finger—the spinning disc of divine discrimination—which severed SwarBhanu's head from his body. Yet because he had tasted immortality, both parts became eternal. The head became Rahu, representing obsession, ambition, and future-oriented consciousness. The body became Ketu, representing past-life attainments, spiritual wisdom, and detachment.

The shadow planets Rahu and Ketu have no physical mass but represent the mathematical points where the Moon's orbit intersects Earth's orbital plane around the Sun. These are called the North Node (Rahu) and South Node (Ketu) of the Moon.

Modern science confirms that these nodal points do indeed represent areas of "churned up electromagnetic energy," as the text describes. The gravitational interactions at these points create subtle but measurable effects on Earth's energy field.

Personal Chart Analysis

The Shrapit Yoga Configuration: The combination of Rahu and Saturn in the same house creates what Vedic astrology calls "cursed yoga"—not because it brings misfortune, but because it demands intense spiritual work. Saturn represents discipline, structure, and karmic lessons, while Rahu represents obsession, innovation, and material desires.

First House Significance: The first house governs:
- **Conscious Identity**: How we see ourselves and present to the world
- **Physical Body**: Our vehicle for experiencing and expressing consciousness
- **Life Direction**: The fundamental thrust of our incarnation

- **Ego Development**: The necessary but eventually transcendable sense of separate selfhood

Scorpio Rising: The sign of Scorpio governing the first house adds layers of complexity:

- **Transformation**: Kundalini rising
- **Intensity**: Everything is experienced with passionate depth
- **Mystery**: Hidden motivations and psychological complexity
- **Power**: The capacity for both destruction and regeneration
- **Investigation**: Compulsive need to understand hidden truths

The Rahu-Saturn Dynamic: Discipline Meets Obsession

Saturn's Influence: Known as the "Great Teacher," Saturn brings:

- **Structure**: The need for systematic approach to growth
- **Responsibility**: Taking ownership of one's karma and choices
- **Patience**: Learning that meaningful development takes time
- **Restriction**: Limitations that force creative solutions
- **Maturity**: Developing wisdom through experience

Rahu's Influence: The dragon's head contributes:

- **Ambition**: Insatiable hunger for achievement and recognition
- **Innovation**: Thinking outside conventional boundaries
- **Restlessness**: Constant seeking for something more
- **Illusion**: Tendency to be fooled by appearances

- **Acceleration**: Rapid, sometimes chaotic change

The Internal Conflict: These energies create ongoing tension:

- Saturn wants slow, steady progress; Rahu demands immediate results
- Saturn emphasizes tradition and proven methods; Rahu seeks revolutionary approaches
- Saturn counsels patience; Rahu feeds on urgency
- Saturn builds through discipline; Rahu achieves through cleverness

The Seventh House Ketu: Past Life Treasures

Ketu's Position: Located in the seventh house in Taurus, accompanied by Sun and Mercury, Ketu reveals:

Seventh House Themes:

- **Relationships**: How we connect with others and what we seek through partnership
- **Subconscious Projection**: The parts of ourselves we see reflected in others
- **Balance**: Learning to harmonize individual needs with partnership requirements
- **Other-Awareness**: Developing consciousness of perspectives beyond our own

Taurus Influence:

- **Resources**: Both material and spiritual wealth
- **Stability**: The need for security and predictable growth
- **Sensuality**: Appreciation of beauty, comfort, and physical pleasure
- **Persistence**: Steady, determined progress toward goals
- **Values**: Clear understanding of what is truly worthwhile

Solar Conjunction: The Sun with Ketu indicates:

- **Creative Spirituality**: Past-life development in artistic

or leadership areas
- **Ego Transcendence**: Learning to express individuality without selfishness
- **Illuminated Detachment**: Wisdom that shines without attachment to results
- **Royal Consciousness**: Natural dignity and noble bearing

Mercury Conjunction: Mercury with Ketu suggests:
- **Intuitive Intelligence**: Knowledge that comes through direct perception
- **Spiritual Communication**: Ability to express transcendent truths
- **Past-Life Learning**: Accumulated wisdom from previous incarnations
- **Manifestation Skills**: Power to bring ideas into material reality

The Symbolic Language of Rahu and Ketu

Rahu as the Sifter: This tool separates valuable grain from worthless chaff, representing:
- **Discrimination**: Learning to distinguish between helpful and harmful influences
- **Purification**: Removing obstacles to spiritual progress
- **Selection**: Choosing which experiences deserve attention and energy
- **Refinement**: Gradually improving the quality of consciousness

Ketu as the Flag: This symbol indicates:
- **Destination**: The goal of spiritual evolution
- **Victory**: Achievement of past-life objectives
- **Guidance**: Direction for current-life development

- **Surrender**: Releasing attachment to ego-driven goals

The Integration Process: Reuniting the Dragon

Raising Rahu's Energy: The transformation from material to spiritual focus involves:

Material Rahu Manifestations:
- Compulsive ambition for status and recognition
- Addiction to stimulation and novelty
- Fear-based grasping for security
- Illusion that external achievements bring fulfillment

Spiritual Rahu Manifestations:
- Passionate dedication to truth-seeking
- Innovative approaches to spiritual practice
- Fearless questioning of limiting beliefs
- Desire for genuine transformation rather than superficial change

Empowering the Seventh House Combination: Working with Sun-Mercury-Ketu in Taurus requires the digging up of hidden talents, compliments of Ketu:

- **Creative Expression**: Using artistic abilities to serve spiritual purposes
- **Relationship Wisdom**: Learning from partnerships without losing individual identity
- **Resource Management**: Developing abundance consciousness that serves others
- **Communication Skills**: Expressing spiritual insights in accessible language

The Kundalini Connection: Serpent Power Ascending

The Spine as Sacred Geography: The process of reuniting

Rahu and Ketu parallels the classical description of Kundalini awakening.

The Third Eye Opening: When the dragons head is reunited with its torso, consciousness achieves:

- **Integrated Vision**: Seeing past, present, and future as unified wholeness
- **Transcendent Knowledge**: Understanding that operates beyond logical thinking
- **Cosmic Awareness**: Recognizing individual identity as part of universal consciousness
- **Practical Wisdom**: Ability to navigate material world with spiritual understanding

This is the splendor of radiance (SwarBhanu) that represents the goal of human evolution: the complete integration of all aspects of being into a unified, conscious, and compassionate whole.

CHAPTER 15

Brihaspati, Teacher of the Gods

Four years had passed since the September 11th attacks forever changed the landscape of international travel and global consciousness. It was August 2, 2005, 1:00 AM, and Ontario International Airport in Canada hummed with the subdued energy of late-night arrivals. After an exhausting flight from Chicago, I found myself among five other single, dark-skinned men, all singled out from the stream of arriving passengers and directed to a sterile holding room for what would prove to be a life-altering interrogation.

The previous 24 hours had been a blur of anticipation and travel fatigue. From my home in paradise—Maui, Hawaii—I had taken the circuitous route through Chicago, spending a restless night in an airport hotel, all for one purpose: to meet the man who would become my spiritual teacher, my guru. The immigration form I had filled out honestly stated my reason for visiting Canada: "to study palmistry." Little did I know that this simple declaration, combined with my appearance and the heightened security climate of post-9/11 America, would set in motion a series of events that would test my resolve and reveal the mysterious workings of karma.

The holding room at Ontario International Airport was a study in institutional bleakness—harsh fluorescent lighting, uncomfortable wooden benches, and an atmosphere thick with suspicion and bureaucratic power. I sat facing a worn wooden counter behind which stood my interrogator: a middle-aged, tired-looking white man in a crumpled dark blue uniform. His weary demeanor suggested the end of a long shift, but fate had orchestrated this encounter with surgical precision.

"Mrs. Anjali Walia DeSure—I hope I'm pronouncing that correctly," he began, his voice soft but laden with skeptical undertones. "Please tell me the reason for your visit to Canada. I see you started your journey in Maui, Hawaii."

"I've come to study palmistry at the Birla Vedic Center in Chennenville for one week," I replied, anxiety creeping into my voice. "There's actually a driver waiting to pick me up, and he must be wondering why I haven't appeared."

Then came the question that would reveal the cosmic irony of the situation: "What is palmistry?"

As he spoke, he casually flipped through my passport pages with his left hand while his right arm rested motionless on the counter. My eyes, trained by years of interest in palmistry, immediately focused on his hands. What I saw sent a shock through my system—his right hand ended at the wrist. Palm and fingers were completely absent, likely due to a congenital birth defect.

The inner voice exclaimed: "Hai Ram, Anjali! What kind of cosmic test is this? This man's right hand is missing—palm, fingers, and all. Of course, he's clueless about the potential hidden in palms and fingers."

The Symbolic Significance of the Missing Hand

The Right Hand:
- Active consciousness and future potential
- How we interact with the external world
- Our capacity to manifest desires and intentions
- The logical, linear mind and masculine energy

The Left Hand:
- Passive consciousness and inherited traits

- Our inner emotional landscape
- Subconscious patterns and feminine energy
- The intuitive, receptive aspects of being

Steadying my trembling heart with my right hand—the hand he lacked—I attempted to explain: "Palmistry is the study of human hands. The left hand mirrors the right brain hemisphere, while the right hand reflects the left brain."

His visible irritation flared. "What proof do you have of this? Show me the paperwork."

This was 2005, before smartphones revolutionized documentation and communication. I carried only a basic flip phone, hardly adequate for displaying the email correspondence that had brought me here.

"I can show you the email exchange between us, but I don't have formal paperwork," I explained, my frustration mounting. "I read two of his books on palmistry and contacted him directly. He invited me to study at his center. I've already paid tuition and accommodations with my credit card, plus the cost of the car and driver waiting outside. You can verify this with him."

"How did you hear about this place?" His voice rose with suspicion.

The irony was palpable. Here I was, trying to explain my passion for reading hands to a man who possessed only one complete hand—and that one was busy condemning my spiritual quest.

"Please wait here. I'll be back," he said curtly, disappearing into the back office with my dark blue U.S. passport.

Minutes stretched like hours as I stood there. When he finally returned, he stamped a page with the official green entry stamp. Relief flooded through me as he began handing back my passport, but something compelled me to speak.

"I feel sorry for your karma, making me wait so long," I blurted out, the words escaping before my rational mind could stop them.

His response was swift and decisive. "Now you're done for," he mumbled, snatching the passport back and stamping a red "ENTRY DENIED" directly over the green approval stamp.

Then the officer escorted me to another holding room where a kind-faced older woman in a similar uniform inspected my belongings with surprising gentleness. When I tearfully recounted the incident, showing her photographs of my family—Kenneth, Pearl, and Ariell—she disappeared briefly with the photo to plead my case.

Returning with obvious disappointment, she delivered the verdict: "He won't budge. He refuses to allow you entry into Canada."

The same officer who had denied me entry then escorted me to the departure gate for the return flight to Chicago, his left hand gripping my right arm. He remained silent throughout, while I sobbed openly, grief-stricken at the collapse of my carefully planned spiritual pilgrimage.

Back at Chicago O'Hare Airport, I called Kenneth, my husband of twenty years. He immediately suggested abandoning this "crazy idea" and returning home. We had built a successful bed-and-breakfast overlooking the Pacific Ocean on two and a half acres dotted with coconut, mango, guava, papaya, orange, and lime trees. From any external perspective, I had everything—prosperity, family, tropical paradise.

Yet something deeper than comfort or security drove my next decision. Ignoring Kenneth's advice, I purchased another round-trip ticket from Chicago to Ontario International Airport. Twenty-four hours later, I found myself at the same airport, at the same time, facing the same immigration process.

This time, remarkably, I sailed through without incident, finally arriving at my guru's retreat center—tired, emotionally drained.

The contrast between my Hawaiian lifestyle and the Canadian retreat center was stark. Where my B&B offered expansive ocean and mountain views and tropical abundance, the Birla Vedic

Center overlooked a simple lake. The retreat center's modest accommodations forced attention inward, away from sensory gratification.

Ghanshyam Singh Birla sat behind a simple wooden desk in a small room adorned only with portraits of Paramahansa Yogananda and his guru, Swami Sri Yukteswar Giri. These images immediately established the spiritual lineage—Yogananda, who brought yoga to the West, and his enlightened teacher who embodied the integration of ancient wisdom with modern understanding.

Birla possessed the unmistakable presence of an authentic spiritual teacher: His black eyes conveyed warmth and understanding that transcended mere intellectual knowledge. He smiled without showing his teeth. Like many advanced practitioners, his joy expressed itself quietly, without display or drama. His receding hairline and simple demeanor reflected the ego-transcendence characteristic of genuine teachers. Despite his unassuming appearance, his presence commanded immediate focus and attention.

Before our consultation, a young assistant had me place both hands in black ink and make clear impressions on white paper. I also completed a detailed questionnaire covering birth information, immigration dates, marriage dates, and children's birthdays. This thoroughness demonstrated the integration of multiple Vedic sciences: palmistry, astrology, and numerology.

"Anjali ji, so finally you are here," Ghanshyam ji said with a gentle smile that never quite revealed his teeth—a characteristic I would learn to associate with profound inner contentment.

"Ghanshyam ji, I've read both your books—'Love in the Palm of Your Hands' and 'Destiny in the Palm of Your Hand.' I'm a devoted fan," I gushed, holding my hands in Anjali mudra near my heart.

"First and foremost, I must inform you that your birth time is incorrect. You were born later than 6:45 PM. You're Scorpio rising, not Libra rising. You have intense, hypnotic eyes."

"I make my assessment based on both palm lines and the birth chart," he explained while intently studying my handprints. "The chart reveals what you bring into this life from previous incarnations. The palm shows all your experiences—tears and triumphs, childhood influences, present mental makeup, willpower, and the actions you choose to take."

"Anjali ji, you were a powerful queen in one of your previous lives, but many people resented you. In this life, you must first become the queen of your own consciousness before receiving appreciation from others."

This statement carried profound psychological and spiritual insights:

The Queen Archetype:
- Represents natural leadership abilities and regal bearing
- Indicates past-life experience with power and responsibility
- Suggests karmic lessons around authority and humility
- Points to the need for inner sovereignty before external recognition

The Resentment Pattern:
- Past-life abuse of power creating current-life obstacles
- The need to earn respect through service rather than demand it through position
- Understanding that external opposition often reflects internal conflicts
- The importance of transforming ego-driven leadership into spiritually motivated guidance

Inner Sovereignty First:
- The recognition that true power comes from self-

mastery
- External validation becomes unnecessary when inner authority is established
- The queen of consciousness rules through wisdom, not force
- Personal transformation must precede social recognition

That first night in my modest room overlooking the lake, jet lag and spiritual excitement combined to create a restless sleep filled with vivid dreams. The most significant vision came in the "sandhi state" between sleeping and waking. I was drowning in the lake outside my window, struggling desperately while Ghanshyam ji and his assistants stood on the shore, observing my plight. They offered no assistance, simply witnessing my struggle with neutral awareness.

Upon waking, I immediately understood the message from my subconscious: "Anjali, you will have to do all the heavy lifting yourself. Don't expect anyone else to save you."

The Guru points the way, but the disciple must walk the path. Advanced spiritual teachers understand that rescuing students from their struggles impedes growth. Like a butterfly that must fight its way out of the cocoon to develop the strength for flight.

In Vedic astrology, Jupiter represents the guru principle within human consciousness. This planet governs:

- **Higher Learning**: Education that transforms the soul, not just the mind
- **Spiritual Wisdom**: Understanding that transcends mere intellectual knowledge
- **Divine Grace**: The mysterious force that brings teacher and student together
- **Expansion**: Growth in consciousness, compassion, and cosmic understanding
- **Dharma**: Living in alignment with universal principles

and personal purpose

Activating Jupiter: According to Vedic teaching, Jupiter remains dormant in the birth chart until activated through finding and learning from a genuine guru. This activation process involves:

- **Recognition**: Identifying authentic spiritual authority versus false teachers
- **Surrender**: Releasing ego-driven resistance to guidance
- **Service**: Offering gratitude and assistance to the teaching lineage
- **Application**: Implementing received wisdom in daily life
- **Transmission**: Eventually sharing learned wisdom with others ready to receive it

CHAPTER 16
Complex Post Traumatic Stress Disorder

A few months passed since my mother's peaceful departure into the astral realms. She lived with us till her soul flew away in an instant at age 84, while enjoying lunch with her good Indian friends in Gig Harbor. I had looked at her palm several times and each time she would ask, "please tell me if will go quickly or suffer for months in a nursing home."

I told her the truth several times, "Ma, your lifeline ends with a clean fork. You will not suffer."

At fifty-eight, I found myself trapped in a daily ritual of psychological torment that began each morning with the same haunting vision.

As consciousness reluctantly returned each dawn, I would envision a magnificent white elephant—eyes kind and fringed with dark, long lashes like those of a gentle giant from ancient Indian tales. This majestic creature would deliberately place one massive foot upon my heart. Then, with a grace that made the gesture even more poignant, it would lift its trunk in what appeared to be a farewell salute to my departing soul.

Each new day arrived not as a gift of possibility but as a predetermined sentence of misfortune. Above my head, I could sense the gathering storm clouds of guilt, regret, and shame—a toxic trinity that had followed me across decades and continents.

"If only Pearl and Ariell were smarter and prettier..." The thought would begin its familiar circuit through my consciousness.

"If only Kenneth was a better businessman..."

"If only I hadn't made so many mistakes..."

Our daughter Ariell had just completed her first year of medical school, and her clinical training was already sharpening her diagnostic instincts.

On this afternoon, she sat across from me at our custom-crafted rectangular dining table made from mango wood with live edges—a piece that Kenneth had commissioned from a local Hawaiian artisan. The natural beauty of the wood, with its flowing organic borders, seemed to mock the artificiality of my constructed misery.

Ariell's hands rested firmly on the table's polished surface as she spoke in an authoritative tone: "Mom, it's time you had a proper diagnosis."

My eyebrows raised involuntarily—a reflexive response that had become legendary within our household. This facial expression served as an early warning system, alerting all family members to my shifting emotional weather.

"Oh... watch out, Mom's going crazy," Ariell said, her hands instinctively cupping her face in a gesture that combined exasperation with genuine concern.

But then her medical training took over, and her voice softened with professional compassion tinged with personal love: "Mom, I love you and want you to get better. Can I please make an appointment for you?"

She leaned across the table, her long fingers gently caressing my cheek.

My left fingers automatically moved to rub my chin—another unconscious gesture that accompanied deep contemplation. In that moment, the inner voice spoke with unmistakable clarity: "You know she's right. Let her make the appointment because I don't trust you will."

My lips puckered into a kiss that I blew toward Ariell with my left hand—a gesture of surrender disguised as affection.

"Okay, beti Lal," I said, using the Hindi endearment that meant "precious daughter." "Make the appointment. Dad will drive me."

My confession that I didn't trust my highway driving skills revealed how depression had eroded my confidence in basic life functions. What had once been routine—navigating freeways, making decisions, trusting my reflexes—now felt impossibly complex and dangerous.

The sixth floor of Kaiser Permanente Medical Center had fluorescent lighting and a cold feel. Dr. Sternback sat across from me behind a modern metal desk. His view was of the Olympic Mountains, their snow-capped peaks offering a majestic backdrop. My view consisted of a gray carpeted bulletin board above his head, covered with notes of various shapes and sizes, secured with black pins—a visual metaphor for the fragmented thoughts and memories that covered the bulletin board of my own consciousness.

Dr. Sternback shared a surname with my second ex-husband Mahesh's colleague in Los Angeles—also a psychiatrist. But this Dr. Sternback appeared twenty or more years older.

His Jewish features resonated with particular significance, given that both my daughters carried Jewish genes intermingled with their East Indian heritage. In that moment, I felt pleased with Ariell's choice.

"Dr. Sternback, I'm only here because my daughter insisted, I see you," I began with characteristic directness.

His response carried the measured cadence of decades of psychiatric practice: "Mrs. DeSure, tell me about yourself." He cleared his throat before adding what would prove to be a crucial detail: "I must inform you that I'm retiring at the end of this month. I won't be able to see you after this visit."

My internal commentator immediately seized upon this limitation: "Good for you, Anjali. It's a great excuse to tell Ariell. You don't have to see him again."

Looking into Dr. Sternback's faded blue eyes, I smiled with genuine appreciation: "I'm so thrilled that you could see me."

Three decades of psychiatric consultations had taught me to distill my complex history into digestible portions. Like a traumatic reduction sauce.

"I'm a victim of childhood sexual abuse and neglect. I grew up in India, where I was abused in the name of religion by our trusted family servant."

I removed my glasses and rubbed my eyes. "I married at age twenty-one, primarily to come to the USA. According to Indian standards, this was considered an excellent match. I met him at the company where I worked as a receptionist—he was the general manager's only son."

"I had a Bachelor of Science degree in Chemistry. He possessed an engineering degree and master's in business, working as a manager at a steel plant in California."

"I met and married him within a month of our first meeting. After three months of cohabitation in the US, I left to live in the dormitory at California State University in Pomona."

This stark timeline concealed the emotional chaos of those early weeks—the desperate attempt to be a wife without understanding what marriage meant, the cultural confusion of American expectations versus Indian conditioning, and the growing awareness that changing continents couldn't change internal landscapes.

"I didn't know how to be a wife or how to please a man. I was so unhappy within myself—so full of fear, doubt, shame, and guilt for something I must have done in past lives."

"It's not like he was the only choice. There were others, but he was the only one living in the US. I was considered a hot commodity, even though my skin is dark."

After my first divorce, I worked diligently for several years to save money to bring my remaining family from India. I dated several men before collapsing into what I now recognize was severe depression.

"That's when I saw the advertisement in India Abroad, published monthly to service expatriates: 'Harvard-trained psychiatrist desires charming life companion. Caste no bar, divorced status acceptable.'"

"I married Mahesh within a month of meeting him. I had been married to Mahesh for a year when I met Kenneth, my present husband. I first encountered him as a patient—he was my chiropractor who cured me of lifelong sinus infections and headaches."

"Kenneth insisted I see his psychiatrist friend, Richard Rosen. I was twenty-nine and on the verge of suicide because I felt nothing good would ever come to me, even though Kenneth loved me madly and was devoted to me."

"Dr. Rosen inquired about my childhood and all household members. After I finished describing Jagdish, the floodgates opened. The stench of truth made my stomach wrench."

"Dr. Rosen hit the nail on its head when he announced: 'You are a textbook case of childhood sexual abuse.'"

Staring at the shiny surface of Dr. Sternback's desk, I scratched my right ear—another unconscious self-soothing gesture—and continued my abbreviated life story:

"You see, I was twenty-nine when I became conscious of the childhood trauma. I had my first child at thirty-one, my second at thirty-three. Thus began my pursuit of motherhood and materialism, which I thought would make me whole."

"I have been fighting fires all my life. Now I feel stuck. I don't like who I've become—always threatening my husband to leave and run away, just like I did in childhood. But back then nobody cared."

"Now I have two loving daughters and a devoted husband, and I'm desperate to find peace. These feelings of worthlessness want to drown me. I want to bring joy to my family after having tortured them."

As tears silently rolled down my cheeks, I shared what would prove to be a crucial diagnostic clue: "Dr. Sternback, I have a passion for fixing broken objects—for repurposing, kind of like 'trash to treasure.'"

This seemingly innocuous detail revealed profound psychological patterns:

- **Projection**: Seeing in broken objects the same potential for redemption I desperately wanted for myself
- **Control**: Finding agency in physical repair when emotional healing felt impossible
- **Hope**: Believing that transformation was possible, at least for inanimate objects
- **Self-Worth**: Finding value through utility rather than inherent being

Dr. Sternback cleared his throat—a gesture that preceded important professional pronouncements.

"Mrs. DeSure, we now have a new diagnosis for your condition. It's not just depression. It's Complex PTSD."

My eyebrows raised and I bit my lower lip.

"PTSD stands for Post-Traumatic Stress Disorder," Dr. Sternback explained. "The 'complex' designation indicates that your trauma was prolonged, repeated, and occurred during critical developmental periods."

"You've listed that you take 20mg of Prozac daily with no other medications. Is that correct?" he paused, "what about illegal drugs, alcohol, sleeping pills…"

I nodded while blowing my nose, the simple act of nasal congestion representing the body's ongoing stress response. I am surprised that I have not become a drug abuser or alcoholic given that I suffered from a severe eating disorder until recently. Binge eating and then throwing it up."

"I suggest increasing your Prozac from 20mg to 60mg and adding a mood stabilizer. I'm recommending 20mg of Abilify.

How is your sleep?"

"Sleep is my biggest problem. It's very hard to leave the bed. I can stay there for two days straight. I'm always exhausted."

This confession revealed the hell of trauma-related sleep disturbance:

- **Hypervigilance**: Nervous system remains alert even during rest
- **Nightmares**: Sleep becomes associated with vulnerability and terror
- **Dissociation**: Bed becomes refuge from overwhelming reality
- **Depression**: Physical fatigue mirrors emotional exhaustion

As I left Dr. Sternback's office that day, carrying prescriptions for increased medication and the gift of accurate diagnosis, I couldn't have imagined the journey that lay ahead. Complex PTSD diagnosis didn't provide instant healing, but it offered something equally valuable: a roadmap for recovery and the knowledge that my suffering had identifiable causes and proven treatments.

The white elephant of my morning visions would gradually transform from harbinger of doom to symbol of gentle wisdom. The clouds of guilt, regret, and shame wouldn't disappear overnight, but they would begin to reveal the clear sky that had always existed behind them.

I would discover that the passion for repairing broken objects had been preparing me all along for the most important restoration project of all: reclaiming my own life from the wreckage of trauma and transforming it into something not just functional, but beautiful.

Traditional PTSD vs. Complex PTSD:

Classic PTSD typically results from a single traumatic incident:

- Combat exposure

- Natural disasters
- Serious accidents
- Violent crimes
- Single instances of abuse

Complex PTSD (C-PTSD), by contrast, develops from prolonged, repeated trauma, especially during childhood:

- Chronic abuse (physical, sexual, emotional)
- Severe neglect
- Captivity or imprisonment
- Living in war zones
- Prolonged domestic violence
- Human trafficking

The Neurobiological Impact: Years of chronic trauma literally rewire the developing brain:

- **Hypervigilance**: The nervous system remains perpetually alert to danger
- **Emotional Dysregulation**: Difficulty managing intense feelings
- **Dissociation**: Disconnection from thoughts, feelings, memories, or sense of identity
- **Negative Self-Concept**: Profound feelings of worthlessness and shame
- **Interpersonal Difficulties**: Problems with trust, boundaries, and relationships
- **Loss of Meaning**: Difficulty finding purpose or hope

CHAPTER 17: ORDER IN CHAOS

At sixty-three, I stood at the precipice of my third marriage, wrestling with the familiar demons of mental illness that had stalked me through decades of supposed healing. Ken and I had built what appeared to be a beautiful life together—raising two daughters who had grown into compassionate, capable women—yet I found myself drowning in an ocean of sorrow so vast that even the occasional moments of joy felt like cruel mockery. They would surface briefly, these golden bubbles of hope, only to burst against the relentless tide of despair.

Each morning brought with it the whisper of the ultimate escape: freeing my soul from the *sthula sharira*, the gross physical body composed of earth, water, fire, air, and space—the five elements that Hindu philosophy teaches bind us to this earthly plane. The forbidden option, once unthinkable, now beckoned with the promise of finally silencing the cacophony of pain that had become the soundtrack of my life.

The irony was not lost on me. Here I was, surrounded by all the trappings of American success—a comfortable home, financial security, a loving family—yet feeling more trapped than I had as a young immigrant girl surviving on ramen noodles and prayers. Countless visits with therapists, their diplomas hanging like trophies on sterile office walls, had yielded little more than empty platitudes. The rainbow of pills—serotonin enhancers, mood stabilizers, anxiety dampeners—sat in my medicine cabinet like colorful promises of normalcy that never delivered. Endless sessions of crying that invariably erupted into volcanic bursts of rage had become my ritual.

All of it pointed to a flashing red sign that I could no longer ignore: "Stop squirming. Look within."

My inner voice cried out with growing urgency: "All those high-priced therapy sessions where you dissected your past with surgical precision, all those prescriptions that promised chemical salvation, all those long-distance moves where you thought geography could outrun your ghosts, all those relationships where you sought completion in another's arms, all those monetary symbols of success that were supposed to validate your worth—even the hand-picked father of your two children, chosen with such careful deliberation—and you still feel unsafe at all times, just like you did in childhood. What is lacking?

I grew up in New Delhi during the tumultuous 1970s, when the very air seemed thick with dreams of escape. Every middle-class Indian family I knew harbored the same golden fantasy: America, the land of abundance where milk and honey flowed in supermarket aisles. The images that reached us through magazines and movies painted a picture of endless possibility—wide highways, gleaming cities, and people who smiled with teeth so white they seemed to glow.

So, when opportunity knocked in the form of marriage proposals, I took what seemed like the easiest path available. Several unsolicited offers were flowing my way, a phenomenon that puzzled me given my dark complexion—a feature that in 1970s India was considered more liability than asset. Yet somehow, some exotic essence seemed to seep through my skin, drawing suitors like moths to a flame. Perhaps it was the way my eyes held depths that spoke of old souls and ancient sorrows, or maybe it was simply the desperation that clung to me like sandalwood perfume.

The timing couldn't have been more providential. My father had passed away just a few years earlier, leaving behind three children and a mother who struggled to keep our small family afloat. As the eldest, I felt the weight of responsibility pressing down on my shoulders. These marriage proposals weren't just romantic opportunities—they were lifelines thrown to a drowning family.

I married a stranger on a warm Delhi night, exactly one month after our first meeting. The entire courtship, if it could be called that, consisted of a few chaperoned conversations and a formal exchange of biodata—those clinical summaries of education, family background, and marriageable assets that served as Indian Cupid's arrows.

He was twenty-eight years old, a highly eligible bachelor and the only son of well-to-do parents who spoke Punjabi and belonged to our caste. The package deal included all expenses paid, a one-way airline ticket to the United States, and most precious of all, a green card that promised a fresh start in the land of dreams.

As I sat in that airplane, watching the subcontinent shrink beneath me until it became nothing more than a brown smudge against blue, I was blissfully clueless about the hefty price that would be extracted from me.

America revealed itself to be everything I had imagined and nothing I had prepared for. Stores sprawled across every corner like temples to capitalism, their aisles groaning under the weight of choices that seemed almost violent in their excess. Twenty varieties of cereal. Eight different types of toothpaste. Mountains of shiny objects whose purpose I couldn't fathom but whose allure was undeniable.

But it was the casual kindness of strangers that truly overwhelmed me. "Hello!" they would chirp, as if my presence mattered to them. "Have a nice day!" they would call after me, their voices carrying genuine warmth. This stood in stark contrast to the reserved formality of Delhi, where strangers maintained careful distance and smiles were currency reserved for those within your social circle.

Yet for all of America's material richness, I felt spiritually bankrupt. No home in any meaningful sense. No familiar faces to anchor me to my own identity. No friends to share the small daily victories and defeats that make up a life. No means of support beyond my own trembling determination. I was like a white feather caught in a hurricane, getting dirty with each downfall, blown from place to place with no agency over my own trajectory.

The marriage that had promised salvation revealed itself within three months to be another form of prison. My husband's criticisms cut deep, not because they were particularly creative, but because they echoed the voice of self-doubt that had always whispered in my ear. I was acting like a preadolescent, he said. I needed to grow up, he insisted.

When my patience finally crumbled, I made the terrifying decision to exit the marriage. It felt like jumping off a cliff with no parachute, but staying felt like a slower form of death.

California State University Pomona became my sanctuary. I secured a shared room in the student dormitory with an incoming freshman whose boundless optimism served as a daily reminder that hope was still possible. The part-time job in the library, stacking books with methodical precision, became a form of meditation. The scholarship for programming and marketing courses felt like a golden ticket to reinvention.

Unlike in India, my dark skin was welcomed in California with open arms and genuine curiosity. "Where did you get this incredible tan?" people would ask, their voices tinged with envy. "What is that beautiful shiny object on your nose?" It was 1978, before yoga studios sprouted on every corner and nose piercings became as common as coffee shops.

Not having the luxury to pay for proper driving lessons, I would only date guys who owned cars with automatic transmissions and possessed both the patience and willingness to teach me to drive.

On mornings when depression wrapped around me like a heavy

blanket and the very thought of sunlight felt like torture, I would sing myself into existence: "If you could see tomorrow the way it looks to me today, you'd say incredible, Anjali, you're incredible." I had shamelessly plagiarized this mantra from a Ford commercial, simply replacing the car manufacturer's name with my own. It was a small act of rebellion against despair, and it worked just often enough to keep me moving forward.

This self-administered musical therapy eventually got me out of bed consistently enough to afford gas for my first car: an orange Honda Civic hatchback with a manual five-speed transmission that had clearly seen better decades. She was a temperamental old lady who demanded patience and offered personality in return. Despite several dangerous encounters—a near-miss with a semi-truck on I-405—she kept me safe with the fierce protectiveness of a guardian angel.

Ultimately, she took her final breath on a dark night along the Riverside Freeway, about thirty-five miles from my tiny apartment. She had carried me through the most vulnerable period of my American journey, asking for nothing more than regular oil changes and the occasional kind word.

During these lean years, my diet consisted primarily of Kraft Macaroni and Cheese—that neon-orange comfort food that tasted like childhood even though I'd never had it as a child—ramen noodles that required only boiling water and hope, and when finances permitted, dark chocolate chip cookies from my favorite vending machine. These small indulgences felt like acts of self-love in a world that often seemed determined to break me down.

Years later, as I sat in the ruins of my mental health , I began to understand that none of it had been random. It all boiled down to karma—that intricate web of cause and effect that Hindu philosophy teaches governs every aspect of existence. Each action, each fleeting thought, creates energy that ripples outward like stones thrown into still water, generating reactions from both our inner emotional landscape and the outer world that surrounds us.

Newton's law of motion, which states that every action has an equal and opposite reaction, suddenly revealed itself as more than just physics—it was a fundamental principle of existence. Einstein's theory of relativity, which predicts that energy is never destroyed but only changes form, began to feel like a cosmic joke designed to confuse ignorant, clueless humans who think they can escape the consequences of their choices.

The theory of karma, as presented in ancient Vedic wisdom, presupposes reincarnation—a concept that had always seemed abstractly comforting but became urgently relevant as I contemplated my own mortality. According to this teaching, the physical body perishes but the soul consciousness travels to astral realms, spending time in dimensions beyond our earthly comprehension before choosing its next incarnation.

Hindus and Buddhists agree that this transition period lasts up to forty-nine earth days, during which the soul reviews its past deeds and future desires like a cosmic performance evaluation. Based on this assessment, it chooses to be reborn as any one of 84,000 possible species, ranging from the humble ant to the complex human, depending on its karmic debts and spiritual aspirations.

A human form is considered the most precious of all possible incarnations—the only vehicle capable of leading the soul to realization of ultimate truth, or *moksha*. This knowledge brought both comfort and terror: comfort in understanding that my suffering had purpose, terror in recognizing how much I might have squandered this rare opportunity.

By the time I reached my sixties, I had surrounded myself with all the material trappings that had seemed impossibly out of reach at twenty-one. A nurturing partner who had stood by me through decades of storms. Two daughters who had grown into women of uncommon compassion and capability. A comfortable home filled with books and art and the accumulated treasures of a well-lived life.

Yet the wound in my heart continued to fester, weeping a poison that no external success could neutralize. I made the radical decision to quit everything else and begin the terrifying work of ruthlessly dissecting the old wounds embedded in my heart and body like shrapnel from battles I could barely remember.

I began chanting the Hanuman Chalisa several times each day, letting the ancient Sanskrit syllables roll over my tongue like healing balm. The forty verses dedicated to the monkey god—symbol of strength, devotion, and fearless service—became my lifeline as I dove deeper into the archaeology of my own trauma.

Slowly, painstakingly, I learned to decipher the life patterns mapped out in my Vedic birth chart. The planetary positions at my birth indicated challenges and growth. I studied the telltale signs etched into my palms like a roadmap written in flesh, each line revealing aspects of character and destiny that had been invisible to my younger self.

The work of forgiveness began with my parents. For years, I had carried their neglect like a stone in my chest, feeling the weight of their inability to provide the safety and nurturing every child deserves. As I learned about their childhoods and the traumas they had inherited from their own parents, understanding began to bloom like a flower in winter soil.

They had done their best with the tools they possessed. Their limitations were not malicious but simply human. Despite everything—the emotional distance, the missed opportunities for connection, the ways they had failed to protect me—I realized that I loved them dearly. This love felt like a radical act of forgiveness, not just toward them but toward the very conditions of human existence that make perfect parenting impossible.

Forgiving the servant who had violated my innocence for twelve years proved surprisingly easier. He must have endured a brutal childhood, that shaped him into someone capable of harming a child. Compassion began to dissolve the hatred I had carried like acid in my veins. He was not a monster but a broken human being acting out his own unhealed trauma.

But learning to stop blaming myself for not standing up to him—that remained the most challenging work of all.

Understanding the Architecture of Karma

The experiences were clearly marked in my birth chart, reflecting what Sanskrit texts call *prarabdha* karma—that portion of our total accumulated karma (*sanchit* karma) that we have chosen to experience in our present lifetime. Like withdrawing a specific amount from a vast bank account, we select certain lessons and challenges to work through during each incarnation.

A child, I came to understand, is unable to exercise free will against an adult who causes harm. This represents *dridha*karma—fixed karmic patterns that must simply be endured, like weather systems moving through the landscape of a life. There is no blame in this, no failure of character or strength. Children are meant to be protected, not to protect themselves from those who should be their guardians.

As an adult, however, when I chose to exercise free will to control my emotions and actions, *dridha/adridha* karma—changeable karmic patterns—came into play. Every moment offered choices about how to respond to circumstances, how to break cycles, how to transform inherited pain into wisdom.

Agami karma represents the seeds waiting to ripen in the future, the consequences of past actions that have not yet manifested. Meanwhile, *kriyaman* karma is the new karma being created by our present thoughts and actions, each decision adding to the vast web of cause and effect that shapes our destiny.

This understanding revolutionized my relationship with suffering. Rather than seeing my pain as evidence of cosmic unfairness, I began to recognize it as the soul's curriculum, carefully designed to foster growth and ultimately liberation.

The ancient texts taught me that humans, along with all sentient beings, are constantly subjected to the electromagnetic influence of the nine planets closest to Earth. We receive and transmit electromagnetic waves at all times, our bodies functioning as cosmic radio stations tuned to frequencies we rarely consciously perceive.

We exist simultaneously in multiple bodies: the gross physical form (*sthula sharira*) that we see in mirrors, and the subtle electromagnetic body (*sukshma sharira*) that serves as the blueprint for our physical form. This subtle body contains the legendary seven chakras—energy centers that regulate everything from survival instincts to spiritual transcendence.

At a newborn's first breath, the position of the nine planets within the twelve zodiac constellations maps out the blueprint of their soul's incarnation. But this blueprint is not destiny carved in stone. Through the sheer force of free will, through conscious choice and spiritual practice, we can modify these patterns. We can reach the pinnacle of our desires or drown in self-pity. The choice, ultimately, is ours.

A Vedic birth chart serves as a map of the *sukshma sharira*, revealing not just personality traits and life events but the deeper spiritual curriculum that the soul has chosen for this lifetime.

The Planetary Parliament

The nine planets function like a cosmic parliament, each contributing its influence to the symphony of human experience:

The Sun represents our core brilliance, our essential spark of divinity. It governs our sense of purpose, our vitality, our ability to shine our unique light into the world.

The Moon, closest to Earth, controls the tidal movements of our emotions. Just as it pulls the oceans, it pulls at the watery depths of our feeling nature, creating the ebb and flow of moods that color every experience.

Venus, our desire, sits on the side of Earth closer to the Sun. It governs not just romantic attraction but our ability to appreciate art, music, and most importantly devotion and desire to unite our consciousness with that of the divine.

Mars, our drive and determination, occupies the other side of Earth from Venus. It provides the warrior energy needed to pursue goals, defend boundaries, and transform vision into reality.

Mercury, our power of communication and manifestation, orbits close to the Sun like a cosmic messenger. It governs how we think, speak, and translate inner experiences into outer expression.

Jupiter, positioned beyond Mars, serves as the reservoir of our wisdom and grace. It represents the teacher within, the part of us that seeks meaning, justice, and spiritual growth.

Saturn, the most distant of the classical planets, functions as our cosmic disciplinarian. It creates boundaries, teaches patience, and delivers both rewards and consequences based on our actions.

This accounts for seven planets with physical mass. There are two additional influences on human consciousness: the shadow planets **Rahu** and **Ketu**, mathematical points created by the Moon's orbital relationship with Earth.

Rahu, the north node, represents our obsessions and ambitions—what we must accomplish in this lifetime to achieve fulfillment. It drives us toward new experiences, often with an intensity that borders on compulsion.

Ketu, the south node, embodies past-life talents and spiritual inclinations. It represents what we have already mastered and must now transcend to continue evolving.

The goal is for Rahu to reach Ketu—for our worldly ambitions to merge with our spiritual wisdom. When this integration occurs, the treasures buried in our subconscious mind rise to the surface and unite with our conscious awareness, creating the profound self-acceptance and self-love that mark spiritual maturity.

The forbidden option that once whispered so seductively now seems not just unnecessary but absurd. Why would I abandon this precious human form just as I'm learning to decode its deepest mysteries? Why would I waste this rare opportunity for liberation that may not come again for countless lifetimes?

CHAPTER 18: ARRIVAL OF LAKSHMI

In May of 2017, I signed the papers that would close the most successful chapter of my entrepreneurial life. Maui Ocean Breezes, the bed and breakfast Ken and I had lovingly created on two and a half acres of paradise overlooking the Pacific, was officially sold. What had begun as a dream in June of 1999 was ending not with celebration, but with a mixture of relief and profound loss that I couldn't yet fully comprehend.

The property had been our sanctuary—a place where the trade winds carried the scent of plumeria through open windows, where the sound of waves provided a constant lullaby, and where guests from around the world came to find their own piece of tropical tranquility. We had built something beautiful there that consistently earned five-star reviews and repeat visitors who became friends.

But by 2017, the magic had curdled into stress. Our daughters, Ariell and Pearl, were already established on the US mainland, pursuing their educations and careers far from Maui's small-town atmosphere. The island that had once felt like a protective embrace now seemed to confine rather than nurture them. They needed the energy of cities, the diversity of opportunity that only larger communities could provide.

Ken, too, had lost his enthusiasm for the hospitality business. The six-hour flights from Seattle to Maui had become burdensome, especially as his aging father needed more attention and support. What had once been an adventure—

juggling two residences, living between the islands and the mainland—now felt like an exhausting marathon.

For several years, I had been flying back and forth like a migrating bird, trying to monitor every aspect of the property's upkeep while managing the inevitable drama that comes with live-in caretaker couples. The emotional weight of maintaining standards from thousands of miles away was crushing. My mornings had become rituals of dread, beginning with checking the latest TripAdvisor reviews with the anxiety of a student awaiting test results.

One negative review could ruin my entire day, sending me spiraling into catastrophic thinking: *Maybe now Maui Ocean Breezes will slip to second or third place among the rural B&Bs in Haiku town. Maybe we're losing our edge. Maybe everything we've worked for is crumbling.*

The constant vigilance required to maintain excellence from a distance had become its own form of prison.

Our second home in Gig Harbor, Washington, couldn't have been more different from our Maui paradise. Built by Ken's father upon his retirement, it was a modest two-story structure surrounded by towering evergreen trees that seemed to close in around the property like protective sentinels—or prison walls, depending on one's perspective.

Where Haiku offered year-round sunshine and temperatures that rarely strayed from a perfect 80 degrees, Gig Harbor delivered nine months of cold, persistent rain that seemed to seep into one's bones. The Pacific Northwest's famous gray skies weren't just weather; they were a mood, a state of being that matched my internal landscape with uncomfortable precision.

In some ways, the environment suited my deteriorating mental state perfectly. The perpetual fog provided the ideal backdrop for my own internal weather system: just sit in the gloom all day, sleep for twelve or fourteen hours at a stretch, cry until my eyes felt like sandpaper, and endlessly regurgitate all the mistakes I had made—a mental exercise that served primarily to justify not getting out of bed.

I threw away my phone, that electronic leash that had kept me tethered to the endless demands of running a business. For the first time in years, I didn't care about making money, didn't care about five-star reviews or occupancy rates or profit margins.

I neglected my appearance. Days would pass without brushing my teeth or combing my hair. The woman who had once prided herself on creating beautiful, welcoming spaces for strangers could barely manage basic self-care.

The irony wasn't lost on me: I had spent years ensuring that guests felt pampered and comfortable, yet I couldn't extend the same kindness to myself.

One particularly cold, gray, and cloudy morning—the kind of day when the difference between dawn and dusk feels academic—Lakshmi arrived. She came accompanied by her owner; a woman caught in the emotional wreckage of divorce who was desperately seeking another home for her precious companion.

Ken and Ariell had arranged this meeting despite my vocal protests. I had not grown up with pets. In traditional Indian households of my generation, animals were respected but kept at a distance. The idea of sharing intimate living space with a creature that couldn't be reasoned with, that operated purely on instinct and need, felt overwhelming to someone who could barely manage her own basic requirements.

The dog in question was a fifteen-pound bundle of white fluff whose owner confessed that she barked frequently and was not fully house-trained. To my depressed mind, this sounded less like acquiring a companion and more like volunteering for additional responsibilities I was spectacularly unequipped to handle.

Who needed a small, demanding creature whose bathroom habits were unreliable? I thought. *I could hardly take care of myself.*

But Ken and Ariell had made their decision, guided by some

instinct about what I needed that I was too lost in my own darkness to recognize.

Despite my disapproval, the dog stayed. Ken, displaying the same methodical care he brought to all his projects, purchased expensive organic dog food, a comfortable sleeping enclosure, and invested in sessions with a dog trainer who would teach her basic commands and, hopefully, some semblance of civilized behavior.

The task of naming this creature fell to me, perhaps as a way to encourage some sense of ownership and responsibility. Her previous owner had simply called her "puppy," which seemed both inadequate and impersonal for a being who would be sharing our living space.

Looking at her prominent black eyes—bright, intelligent orbs that seemed almost cartoonishly large as they peered out from her cloud of pure white fur—I first tried "Meenakshi," meaning "the one with beautiful eyes" in Sanskrit. The name felt right intellectually, honoring both her most striking feature and my cultural heritage.

She ignored me completely when I called her by this name, showing about as much interest as she might display toward furniture.

Then, almost without thinking, I tried "Lakshmi, come here."

The transformation was immediate and unmistakable. Her tail began wagging with enthusiasm so that her entire hindquarters wiggled, a semicircle of white hair perched on her back like a jaunty flag. She trotted over and licked my hand.

The synchronicity was too perfect to ignore. The name Lakshmi was profoundly appropriate—the Hindu goddess of wealth, fortune, prosperity, and abundance traditionally wears white and is often depicted surrounded by white lotuses. This little white dog had arrived just days before Diwali, the Festival of Lights, when Hindu families traditionally honor Lakshmi and invite her blessings into their homes.

The fact that I was in no state to celebrate Diwali, or anything else for that matter, only made her timing seem more intentional, as if the universe had decided to deliver its blessings whether I was ready to receive them or not.

The early months of cohabitation tested both our patience and my rapidly fraying sanity. A few months into our arrangement, I found myself fantasizing about wringing her neck and then shooting myself afterward—dark thoughts that scared me with their intensity but felt grimly satisfying to contemplate.

Her pristine white hair seemed magnetically attracted to every dark garment I owned, creating a constant reminder of her presence even when she wasn't in the room. No amount of lint rolling could completely eliminate the evidence of her existence.

Her bathroom habits remained charmingly unreliable. Despite the carefully placed blue pee pads and Ken's patient training efforts, she frequently missed her target and peed on the blue rug next to the door. Whether this was confusion about which blue surface was appropriate or a subtle act of rebellion, I never determined.

Most challenging of all was her insistence on sleeping at the foot of our queen-size bed. Ken seemed unbothered by this arrangement, but I found myself feeling crowded in my own bed, resentful of this uninvited bedmate who slept with the deep contentment of someone who belonged exactly where she was.

Despite my conscious resistance, Lakshmi began to work her way into my heart through a combination of persistence, authenticity, and what I can only describe as shameless emotional manipulation.

Was it the way she would completely relax on the floor, all four paws spread out while lying on her stomach in a position of total vulnerability and trust? This was a creature who had learned to feel safe in our home even when I couldn't feel safe in my own skin.

Or perhaps it was the way she looked at me when I offered her treats—not with the calculating expression of someone working an angle, but with pure, uncomplicated gratitude that made me remember what it felt like to appreciate simple pleasures.

Most disarming of all was her response to my tears. When she found me crying—which was frequently during those dark months—she would gently lick my face and nose with a tenderness that felt almost sacred. There was no judgment in her attention, no attempt to fix or change my emotional state, just presence and acceptance that communicated more comfort than years of therapy sessions.

Later, as I began to emerge from the deepest part of my depression and returned to studying Vedic Astrology, I discovered connections that sent chills down my spine. According to my Vedic birth chart, I was going through the twenty-year planetary cycle of Venus.

Venus, the planet associated with the desire for love, beauty, and relationships, can bring profound lessons about self-worth and the ability to receive affection. Traditional remedies for a difficult Venus period include prayers and offerings to Goddess Lakshmi, the very deity whose name my little companion bore.

Further research revealed even more specific cosmic synchronicity. In my birth chart, Venus was positioned in the *nakshatra* (lunar mansion) of Ardra—the only one among the twenty-seven nakshatras described as "a teardrop turning into a diamond after lots of strife." The imagery was so perfect it took my breath away: transformation through suffering, beauty emerging from sorrow, precious gems forged under pressure.

Each nakshatra has an associated animal that embodies its energy and teachings. The animal connected to Ardra, the teardrop-diamond nakshatra, is a female dog.

As I began to pay closer attention to Lakshmi's daily routines, I realized she was teaching me lessons about living that no human teacher had been able to convey. She was always completely present in the moment, fully engaged with whatever was happening right now rather than worrying about past mistakes or future uncertainties.

She possessed an authenticity that was both admirable and slightly intimidating. When strangers approached, she growled—not from meanness, but from honest assessment of potential threat. When she was excited, her tail wagged with such enthusiasm that her entire body participated in the celebration. When she wanted to show love, she licked faces with generous, sloppy affection that left no doubt about her feelings.

She maintained her physical body with the same attention I once gave to maintaining five-star hospitality standards. She would chew and lick her paws to keep them in optimal condition, grooming herself with the dedication of someone who understood that self-care was not selfish but necessary.

Most remarkably, she never faked a single response. If she didn't want to go for a walk, she would acknowledge my invitation with a polite tail wag and then return to whatever was actually interesting to her at the moment. There was no guilt, no elaborate excuses, no people-pleasing behavior—just honest communication about her current needs and desires.

She taught me that joy could exist in the smallest moments: the arrival of dinner, a sunny patch on the carpet, the sound of a familiar voice. Her capacity for finding pleasure in simple experiences reminded me that happiness didn't require elaborate circumstances or major life changes—sometimes it was as accessible as a belly rub or a comfortable place to nap.

As I watched Lakshmi settle into our home with the confidence of someone who had always belonged there, I began to understand that her arrival marked more than just the acquisition of a pet. She represented the universe's intervention in my healing process, arriving precisely when I needed her most and equipped with exactly the lessons I was ready to learn.

The goddess Lakshmi had indeed come to bless our home, though not in any form I could have anticipated. She arrived wearing white fur instead of silk, communicating through tail wags instead of mantras, teaching presence through example rather than scripture.

In accepting her into my life, I was learning to accept myself back into my own existence—not the version I thought I should be, but the person I actually was, complete with flaws, fears, and the capacity for unexpected joy.

Through her patient presence, authentic responses, and unwavering commitment to living in the moment, she reminded me that transformation often comes in small, daily increments rather than dramatic revelations. She taught me that sometimes the greatest healing happens not through trying to fix what's broken, but through learning to be present with what is.

CHAPTER 19: PANCHANGULI DEVI, GODDESS OF FIVE FINGERS

The Forgotten Goddess

In the vast pantheon of Hindu deities, where gods and goddesses govern everything from the movements of celestial bodies to the sprouting of seeds, there exists a figure whose influence is literally at our fingertips, yet whose name has been largely forgotten by modern practitioners. Panchanguli Devi, the Goddess of Five Fingers, represents one of the most intimate and accessible forms of divine intervention available to human beings.

Unlike the more widely celebrated deities whose images grace temples and home altars, Panchanguli Devi requires no external shrine. She dwells within the architecture of our own hands, presiding over what ancient Vedic texts describe as "the dwelling place of the five elements." Her worship doesn't demand elaborate rituals or expensive offerings, but rather a deep understanding of the electromagnetic symphony that plays constantly within our palms and fingers.

This goddess is intimately connected with Tantra philosophy —not the popular Western misunderstanding of Tantra as merely a sexual practice, but the profound spiritual science that recognizes the human body as a microcosm of the universe itself. In authentic Tantric tradition, every part of the physical form is understood to be a gateway to cosmic consciousness, and the hands represent perhaps the most sophisticated and accessible of these gateways.

The Five Elements

To understand Panchanguli Devi's domain, we must first comprehend the fundamental building blocks of existence as described in Vedic cosmology. According to this ancient system, all of creation—from the vast expanse of galaxies to the smallest atomic particles—emerges from five primary elements that exist in a precise hierarchical relationship.

Akasha (Ether) is the first and most subtle element, the primordial space from which all other elements emerge. It represents potential itself—the pregnant void that contains infinite possibilities. Akasha is not emptiness but rather the fundamental fabric of existence, the cosmic consciousness that underlies all manifestation.

From Akasha arises **Vayu (Air)**, the element of movement and change. Air carries information, sound, and the breath of life itself. It represents the dynamic principle that transforms potential into kinetic energy, the force that sets creation into motion.

Air's friction and movement generate **Agni (Fire)**, the element of transformation and illumination. Fire represents not just physical flame but all forms of energy that create change—digestion, metabolism, intellectual understanding, and spiritual realization. It is the force that breaks down the old to make space for the new.

Fire's cooling creates **Jal (Water)**, the element of cohesion and flow. Water represents the binding force that holds things together, the emotional and intuitive aspects of existence. It is fluid, adaptive, taking the shape of whatever contains it while maintaining its essential nature.

Finally, Water's condensation forms **Prithvi (Earth)**, the element of stability and manifestation. Earth represents the physical realm, the solid foundation upon which all other elements can express themselves. It is matter made concrete, dreams given form.

These five elements don't exist in isolation but rather in constant dynamic relationship, each containing and being contained by the others in an endless dance of creation, preservation, and transformation.

The Sacred Geography of the Hand

When we extend our hand and examine our five fingers, we are looking at a living mandala that maps the entire cosmos. Each finger serves as a conduit for one of the five elements.

The Thumb: Angushtha, King of the Hand

The **thumb**, known in Sanskrit as *Angushtha* ("the king of the hand"), represents the Ether element and stands apart from the other fingers both anatomically and spiritually. Its unique positioning and opposability have been crucial to human evolution, allowing us to manipulate tools and create technology.

The dominance of the human thumb over those of our primate relatives is no evolutionary accident. While chimpanzees and baboons have long fingers and relatively small thumbs, humans have developed this remarkable digit that can touch any other finger with precision. This physical capacity mirrors our spiritual potential—the ability to bring together any combination of elemental energies with conscious intent.

In Ayurvedic understanding, the thumb governs the brain and the nervous system. When we strengthen and focus our thumb's energy, we enhance our mental clarity, decision-making capacity, and overall neurological health.

The Index Finger: Tarjani, the Way-Shower

The **index finger**, called *Tarjani* ("the one who shows the way"), embodies the Air element and serves as our primary tool for pointing, indicating, and directing attention. This finger represents our capacity for guidance, teaching, and leadership. When we point toward something, we are exercising our Air element—using movement and direction to convey information.

Physiologically, Tarjani governs the lungs and respiratory system. The quality of our breathing directly affects the vitality of this finger, and working with this finger through mudra can enhance our breathing capacity and overall respiratory health.

The Middle Finger: Madhyama, the Central Fire

The **middle finger**, *Madhyama* ("the middle one"), holds the Fire element at the center of our hand. As the longest finger, it represents the transformative power that stands at the heart of all change. This finger governs our digestive fire—not just our ability to process food, but our capacity to digest experiences, emotions, and spiritual teachings.

The middle finger's prominence makes it a natural focal point for directing energy. In mudra practice, this finger is often used to channel transformative fire energy for healing and spiritual development.

The Ring Finger: Anamika, the Unnamed Mystery

The **ring finger** presents us with one of the most intriguing aspects of hand symbolism. Its Sanskrit name, *Anamika*, means "the one who cannot be named," indicating its association with the Water element—the most fluid and unpredictable of all elements.

The ring finger represents our emotional nature in all its complexity and unpredictability. This finger governs the kidneys and bladder, the organs responsible for filtering and releasing what the body no longer needs.

Interestingly, this finger appears twice in the Ayurvedic system of doshas (constitutional types). When combined with the little finger (Earth), it represents *Kapha* dosha—the stabilizing, nurturing aspect of our nature. When paired with the middle finger (Fire), it represents *Pitta* dosha—our metabolic fire and capacity for transformation. This dual nature reflects water's ability to either support or extinguish fire, to either stabilize or destabilize earth.

The Little Finger: Kanishtha, the Efficient Finisher

The **little finger**, *Kanishtha* ("the one who gets the job done"), may be the smallest but it represents the Earth element—the foundation upon which all other elements depend. This finger governs the heart, the organ that tirelessly pumps life-sustaining blood throughout our body.

Despite its size, the little finger provides crucial power for gripping and remarkable precision for writing. It represents our capacity to manifest dreams into physical reality, to take abstract concepts and give them concrete form.

The Science Behind the Sacred

Modern neuroscience has validated many aspects of ancient hand wisdom in ways that would have seemed miraculous to our ancestors. Dr. Wilder Penfield's groundbreaking research in the 1930s resulted in the creation of the sensory and motor homunculus—a map showing how much brain space is devoted to controlling different parts of the body.

The results were startling: the hands occupy more brain real estate than any other part of the body except the mouth and tongue. This massive neural investment reflects the hands' crucial role in human development and consciousness. The right hand mirrors the left brain (associated with logic, language, and analytical thinking) while the left hand mirrors the right brain (associated with creativity, intuition, and holistic perception).

An adult human skeleton contains 206 bones, and remarkably, 54 of these—more than a quarter—are located in the hands and wrists. The feet, by comparison, contain 52 bones. Out of 206 bones 106 are dedicated to the hands and feet. As the ancient saying goes, "Mother Nature does not waste!"—this skeletal investment in our hands and feet reflects their supreme importance for human survival and evolution.

The Electromagnetic Symphony

According to Ayurvedic understanding, the human body is permeated by countless *nadis*—channels through which *prana* (life force energy) flows. These energy pathways are remarkably similar to what modern science describes as the bioelectrical currents that animate our nervous system.

The landscape of a human palm is constantly being affected by electrical currents flowing to and from the brain. When we strengthen our fingers, increase their flexibility, and improve their posture, we create clearer channels for this bioelectrical communication. The raised areas beneath each finger (called mounts in palmistry) serve as energy centers that can be activated through massage and conscious attention.

Three major nerves control the five fingers:

- The **Median and Radial nerves** work together to control the thumb, index finger, and middle finger
- The **Ulnar nerve** solely controls the little finger

- All three nerves—**Radial, Median, and Ulnar**—collaborate to maintain proper functioning of the ring finger

This neurological arrangement mirrors the water element's role in the doshas: just as the ring finger requires all three nerves for optimal function, water element participates in two out of the three ayurvedic dosha combinations, demonstrating its fluid, adaptive nature.

The Cosmic Hand: Astrology in the Palm

Vedic palmistry reveals that the hand contains not just anatomical structures but an entire astrological chart. The twelve zodiac signs reside on the four fingers across their twelve segments (three segments per finger), while each of the nine planets of Vedic astrology has its designated place on the palm. The top phalange of the thumb represents will power and the bottom phalange represents logic.

This means that every human hand contains a complete map of cosmic influences—a personal mandala that reflects both our karmic inheritance and our latent potential.

When we understand this cosmic geography, we can use specific hand positions (mudras) to influence particular planetary energies or elemental imbalances. Rather than being passive recipients of cosmic influence, we become conscious participants in our own energetic harmony.

The Three Constitutional Types

Ayurveda classifies all human beings according to three fundamental constitutional types or *doshas*, each representing a different combination of elements:

Vata Dosha combines Ether and Air elements, representing the principle of movement and change. Vata types tend to be quick-thinking, creative, and adaptable, but may struggle with anxiety and inconsistency. Their fingers tend to be long and thin, with prominent joints.

Pitta Dosha combines Fire and Water elements, representing the principle of transformation and metabolism. Pitta types are typically focused, intelligent, and goal-oriented, but may struggle with anger and intensity. Their hands are usually medium sized with warm skin and visible veins.

Kapha Dosha combines Water and Earth elements, representing the principle of stability and nourishment. Kapha types are generally calm, nurturing, and steady, but may struggle with lethargy and resistance to change. Their hands tend to be broad and soft with thick, smooth skin.

Understanding your constitutional type allows you to use specific finger combinations in mudra practice to restore balance when one dosha becomes excessive or deficient.

The Secret of Mudras

Hasta mudras (hand gestures) work by creating specific electromagnetic circuits within the hand that influence the flow of prana throughout the body. When we bring certain fingers together in precise configurations, we complete energetic circuits that can enhance healing or restore constitutional balance by manipulating the ratio of the five elements of creation which in turn influence the seven upper chakras.

The effectiveness of mudras depends not just on correct finger placement but on the quality of awareness we bring to the practice. The hands must be flexible, the fingers strong and properly aligned, the wrists mobile and relaxed. But before the hands turn into exquisite fine-tuning tools the seven animal chakras located below the muladhara chakra have to be purified.

Animals in the Wild

Indigenous wisdom traditions around the world have long

observed that animals possess innate healing abilities that humans have largely forgotten.

A wounded animal in the wild doesn't have access to hospitals or pharmacies. Their survival depends on maintaining optimal functioning of their extremities—their primary tools for finding food, building shelter, and defending against predators.

Humans are "animals in the wild" who have forgotten how to listen to our bodies' innate wisdom. Our survival no longer depends on keeping our hands and feet in peak condition, so we've lost touch with their healing potential. We've traded precision and power for convenience, relying on tools and gadgets rather than developing our natural capabilities.

Awakening the Healer Within

Panchanguli Devi's greatest gift is the reminder that we each possess extraordinary healing abilities that require no external technology or intervention. By developing our understanding of the elemental energies flowing through our hands, by practicing mudras with knowledge and devotion, by treating our fingers with the respect due to sacred instruments, we can awaken healing capacities that most people never imagine possible.

The goddess who dwells within our fingertips awaits our recognition. She has been with us since birth, patiently offering her gifts through every gesture we make, every touch we share, every creative act we perform with our hands. In honoring Panchanguli Devi, we honor the divine potential that literally rests in our own palms.

Through conscious relationship with this forgotten goddess, we can transform our hands from mere appendages into instruments of healing, creativity, and spiritual awakening. We can learn to read the cosmic messages written in our palms, to channel elemental energies through our fingers, and to participate consciously in the electromagnetic symphony that connects us to all of creation.

This is the true worship of Panchanguli Devi—not through elaborate ceremonies or expensive offerings, but through awakening to the sacred technology that has been ours all along, hidden in plain sight at the ends of our arms, waiting for us to remember who we truly are.

CHAPTER 20: THE HUMAN FORM, A TOOL FOR TANTRA

The Precious Vessel...A Living Temple

To be born in a human body is as rare as a blind turtle popping its head through a wooden ring in the midst of a turbulent ocean.

This ancient Buddhist metaphor, echoed across centuries of spiritual teachings, captures a truth that modern consciousness has largely forgotten. In a universe where countless forms of life exist—from the microscopic bacteria that thrive in volcanic vents to the vast intelligences that may inhabit distant galaxies—the human form represents the perfect vessel for spiritual transformation.

According to Vedic cosmology, among the 8.4 million species of life, only us humans possesses the precise combination of consciousness, free will, and physical structure.

Understanding Tantra: Beyond Popular Misconceptions

In the West, Tantra has been reduced to a collection of exotic sexual techniques, but this represents perhaps the greatest misunderstanding of one of humanity's most sophisticated spiritual sciences. Tantra involves the practice of awakening energy located in the muladhara chakra and directing it to rise through the central channel known as the Sushumna. This channel passes through each chakra and culminates at the top of the head in the thousand-petaled lotus.

Tantra, derived from the Sanskrit roots *tan* (to expand) and *tra* (tool or technique), is literally "the tool for expansion"—specifically, the expansion of consciousness beyond its ordinary limitations. Rather than rejecting the material world as an illusion to be transcended, Tantra recognizes the physical universe, including the human body, as manifestations of divine consciousness itself.

The ultimate goal of Tantra is the awakening of *Kundalini*—the dormant spiritual energy that lies coiled at the base of the spine like a serpent of latent potential. This energy is often depicted as a black snake with three and a half coils, sleeping in the *Muladhara* chakra, waiting to be awakened and guided upward to unite with *Shiva* consciousness at the crown of the head.

Unlike many spiritual traditions that require renunciation of the world or adherence to strict moral codes, Tantra offers what might be called a "democratic path"—one that is accessible to individuals living ordinary human lives. The human body becomes the laboratory, everyday experiences become the curriculum, and awakening becomes possible without withdrawal from the world

The Sacred Architecture of the Human Form

The ancient rishis (seers) who developed Tantric science understood the human form not as a random product of evolutionary forces, but as a carefully designed instrument for consciousness transformation based on the fact that Macrocosm resides in the Microcosm

The Principle of Bilateral Symmetry

Bilateral symmetry—the mirror-image correspondence

between the left and right sides of the human form when disturbed can lead to malfunctioning of the ancient reptilian brain which in turn disrupts the ideal state of the survival based consciousness.

Modern neuroscience has validated aspects of this ancient understanding. Dr. Onur Güntürkün of the Institute of Cognitive Neuroscience at Ruhr-University Bochum in Germany has demonstrated that asymmetries in human form can provide crucial diagnostic information about the underlying causes of dysfunction and disease. When the bilateral symmetry of the human form is disrupted—particularly in pelvic alignment due to accident or chronic trauma—the entire energetic system can become imbalanced.

The left side of the body is associated with the lunar, feminine principle (*Ida* nadi), governing intuition, receptivity, and the subconscious mind. The right side embodies the solar, masculine principle (*Pingala* nadi), governing logic, action, and conscious awareness. The central channel (*Sushumna* nadi) represents the integration of these polarities—the pathway through which Kundalini travels to achieve union with divine consciousness.

This disruption of bilateral symmetry affects not only the seven primary chakras but also what Tantric texts describe as the seven "animal chakras" located below the *Muladhara* between the pelvis and the soles of the feet. These lower energy centers connect us to our instinctual, survival instinct. When these foundational energies are disturbed, the autonomic nervous system cannot function optimally, creating cascading effects throughout the entire psychophysical system.

The Vitruvian Perfection

The Renaissance master Leonardo da Vinci was inspired to create his famous drawing of the Vitruvian Man based on proportions described by the ancient Roman architect

Vitruvius. This image—of a human figure inscribed within both a circle and a square—represents more than artistic achievement; it captures the mathematical perfection inherent in the human form.

According to Vitruvian proportions, the length of a human foot is 1/6 of total height, while the span of the hands equals 1/10 of height. These are not arbitrary measurements but reflections of the golden ratio and other sacred geometric principles that govern everything from the spiral of galaxies to the arrangement of seeds in a sunflower.

The Chakra System: Stations of Transformation

The chakra system represents the core technology of Tantric transformation—a sophisticated map of consciousness as it manifests through the human energy body. They are not simple energy centers associated with different colors and qualities, they are the complex gateways between different dimensions of existence.

Muladhara: The Foundation of Survival

The journey of Kundalini awakening begins at the *Muladhara* chakra, located at the base of the spine. Here, in what yogic texts describe as a four-petaled lotus, the serpent power lies dormant, coiled three and a half times around a luminous *lingam* (pillar of light) that represents the axis of the world.

Muladhara governs our most fundamental relationship with physical existence—our sense of safety, survival, and belonging. When this chakra is balanced, we feel grounded, secure, and connected to the earth. When disturbed, we experience anxiety, fear, and a sense of existential disconnection.

This chakra has four petals and is the residence of the sense of smell

Svadhisthana: The Realm of Pleasure and Creativity

As Kundalini awakens and begins its ascent, it must first pierce through the *Svadhisthana* chakra, located in the sacral region. This six-petaled lotus governs sexuality, creativity, and our capacity for pleasure and emotional flow.

Svadhisthana represents our relationship with the waters of life—both literal and metaphorical. Here we learn to navigate the currents of desire, emotion, and creative expression. This chakra has six petals and sense of taste resides here.

The piercing of Svadhisthana often involves deep healing around sexuality, creativity, and our relationship with pleasure.

Manipura: The City of Jewels

Upon reaching the *Manipura* chakra at the navel center, Kundalini encounters what texts describe as "the city of jewels"—a ten-petaled lotus that serves as the seat of personal power and transformation. This is where the Sun resides within the human form, the home of the Fire element that purifies individual consciousness and reveals buried emotions.

Manipura represents a crucial stage in the evolution of consciousness. Here, the awakened individual learns to practice their *dharma* (life purpose) by skillfully employing available resources (*artha*). This chakra governs digestion—not only of food but of experiences, emotions, and spiritual teachings.

This process can be intense, as buried emotions and suppressed aspects of the psyche surface to be integrated or released, "learning to maintain the inner fire without being consumed by it".

Anahata: The Unstruck Sound

As consciousness moves higher, it reaches the *Anahata* chakra at the heart center—the twelve-petaled lotus where human love begins to transform into divine love. "Anahata" means "unstruck sound," referring to the celestial music that arises when this chakra is fully awakened.

The piercing of Anahata often involves profound emotional healing and the development of what Buddhism calls *maitri*—unconditional friendliness toward all aspects of existence. This is where many practitioners encounter their deepest wounds around love, belonging, and self-worth.

Vishuddhi: The Purification Center

If the practitioner is fortunate enough to have their Kundalini energy travel to the throat and pierce the *Vishuddhi* chakra, they encounter the purification center that governs communication, creative expression, and the refinement of intellectual understanding (*buddhi*).

Vishuddhi, the sixteen-petaled lotus at the throat and the residence of the Akasha element. Now individual learns to speak and act from authentic wisdom rather than conditioning or ego-driven motivation. This chakra governs not only verbal communication but all forms of creative expression—the capacity to bring inner vision into outer manifestation.

The opening of Vishuddhi often involves confronting patterns of dishonesty, learning to express truth with compassion, and developing the courage to share our authentic gifts with the world.

Ajna: The Command Center

With sustained meditation and grace, Kundalini can reach the *Ajna* chakra between the eyebrows—the two-petaled lotus where the Moon resides and the sixth sense is activated. Ajna is often called the "third eye" or "command center" because from this perspective, the practitioner can perceive the underlying patterns that govern both personal and cosmic existence.

The Mahat Tattva resides here, the mother of the five elements, the Panch Tattva.

The activation of Ajna often brings psychic abilities, prophetic dreams, and insight into the nature of reality. However, traditional teachings warn against becoming attached to these phenomena, which are merely signposts along the path rather than the destination itself.

Sahasrara: The Thousand-Petaled Lotus

The ultimate goal of Kundalini awakening is the union of individual consciousness with universal consciousness at the *Sahasrara* chakra—the thousand-petaled lotus at the crown of the head. Here, Shakti (the creative power that has been rising through the chakras) merges with Shiva (pure consciousness).

This union results in *moksha*—liberation from the illusion of separation and the realization of our true nature as undivided consciousness. The awakened individual recognizes that they have never been separate from the divine.

The Body as Cosmic Computer

Modern neuroscience has begun to validate what Tantric practitioners have known for millennia: the human body is far more sophisticated than we previously imagined. Dr. Paul Bach-y-Rita's groundbreaking research at the University of Wisconsin demonstrated that our senses are remarkably interchangeable. His famous observation—"We see with our brain, not our eyes. Our skin could substitute for a retina"—points toward the extraordinary plasticity and potential of human neurology.

This research reveals what Ayurvedic physician Dr. Vasant Lad has long taught: "Every cell is a center of consciousness." If consciousness exists at the cellular level, then every part of the human body possesses intelligence and the capacity for storing and processing information—including emotional information.

This understanding transforms our relationship with physical symptoms and illness. Rather than viewing the body as a machine that occasionally breaks down, we begin to recognize it as a sophisticated feedback system that constantly communicates the state of our consciousness. Physical symptoms become messages from our cellular intelligence, opportunities for greater awareness and integration.

The Skin as Universal Sensor

As our largest sense organ, the skin possesses remarkable capabilities that modern science is only beginning to understand. Beyond its obvious functions of protection and temperature regulation, the skin can smell, touch, taste, see, and hear in ways that bypass our traditional sensory organs. The skin when touched stimulates the Air element residing in the Anahata chakra, the heart chakra.

If the skin can function as a "retina," then the entire surface of the human body becomes a potential organ of perception. Tantric practices that involve conscious touch, massage, and energetic healing work, recognize that our skin, especially the soles of our feet and our palms have direct connections with the subconscious mind which resides in our Sukshma sharira or our subtle body.

.

CHAPTER 21: MA KALI, THE TRANSFORMER

It was six months after COVID-19 swept across the globe like a dark tide, shutting down everything we had taken for granted. In this strange new landscape of masks and social distancing, I found myself diving into the shadows of my own psyche. The enforced stillness acted like a magnifying glass, intensifying every aspect of myself I had avoided through years of busyness and external accomplishment.

It was during this time of global reckoning that my friend Gwen flew into my life like an angel bringing a magic potion she had brewed for herself. I had first met her in the Apple store in Tacoma WA. Gwen had grown up in the segregated neighborhoods of New York, where survival required a different kind of strength than what I had learned in the drawing rooms of New Delhi. An emergency nurse who had spent decades witnessing human suffering in its rawest forms, she carried within her lineage the ancient wisdom of Santeria—that powerful synthesis of Yoruba spirituality, Catholic mysticism, and Caribbean magic that had sustained her ancestors through centuries of oppression.

We were both experiencing similar symptoms during those isolating months: a persistent anxiety that felt like drowning while awake, insomnia that made nights stretch into eternity, and a bone-deep fatigue that no amount of rest could heal. More significantly, we shared the invisible wounds that so many women carry—histories of childhood sexual abuse that had shaped our nervous systems, our capacity for trust, our relationship with our own bodies.

Gwen had discovered that small doses of marijuana tincture, prepared according to recipes passed down through her spiritual lineage, could temporarily unlock the frozen places in her nervous system where trauma had crystallized causing chronic symptoms.

One gray afternoon as we sat six feet apart in my garden, watching the roses I had planted years ago continuing to bloom despite the chaos surrounding us. My inner voice taunted me, "Why don't you learn from these flowers. Every day they open up and bloom, aware of the fact that they are so fragile and their life story is so short, spreading their scent and joy all around.

She shared her homemade tincture with me—a dark, bitter liquid that tasted of earth and possibility.

I would place ten drops into a small glass of fresh orange juice or ruby-red pomegranate juice, watching the dark medicine swirl and disappear into the lighter liquid and then gulp it down.

Within thirty minutes, a profound relaxation would spread through my muscles—not the heavy, numbing effect I had expected, but rather a gentle releasing that felt like my body finally exhaling a breath it had been holding for over fifty years. This wasn't escape from my symptoms but rather a heightened awareness of them, as if a veil had been lifted between my conscious mind and the cellular memory stored in my tissues.

When I practiced yoga after taking the medicine, I could feel every muscle respond and communicate with me in ways that had been impossible before. My right hip would whisper stories of the fear I had carried since childhood. My shoulders would release tensions that spoke of decades of trying to be strong enough to never be hurt again. My throat would open and tell me about all the words I had swallowed rather than speak my truth. The knot in my stomach would dissolve and my digestion would greatly improve.

During this period of expanded awareness, I devoured books on trauma healing with the hunger of someone who had finally found water source after decades of wandering in the desert. Two works particularly spoke to me: "In an Unspoken Voice" by Dr. Peter Levine and "The Body Keeps the Score" by Dr. Bessel van der Kolk.

Dr. Levine's work on Somatic Experiencing revealed how trauma becomes trapped in the nervous system, creating symptoms that persist long after the original danger has passed. His research showed that healing trauma wasn't primarily about talking through memories but about teaching the nervous system to release the frozen survival responses that were holding the nervous system captive long after the trauma had passed.

Dr. van der Kolk's comprehensive exploration of how trauma literally reshapes both body and brain provided the scientific validation for what ancient healing traditions had always known: that the body is not just the container for our experiences but the place where transformation must ultimately occur.

I began to form what felt like personal relationships with different parts of my body—greeting my liver each morning, thanking my heart for its tireless service, apologizing to my digestive system for decades of stress-induced neglect. Each organ, each system, each cluster of tissues began to feel like a separate being with its own story to tell and its own wisdom to share.

As my awareness of my body's stored trauma deepened, I found myself drawn to petition the fiercest form of divine feminine energy I knew: Ma Kali, the dark goddess who represents the transformative power that destroys what no longer serves in order to make space for new life.

I began praying to Ma Kali not for comfort or protection, but for the strength to go beyond my current mental and physical limitations. I understood intuitively that what I needed was not gentle healing but radical transformation—the kind that requires the complete death of old patterns before new ones can be born.

Following this inner calling, I began to hold yoga poses and hand mudras for increasingly longer periods of time, learning to breathe calmly with discomfort rather than immediately moving away from it. This wasn't masochistic self-punishment but rather a conscious practice of expanding my capacity to remain present with difficulty. Ultimate goal was to stop my hands and feet from sweating, curing frequent digestive issues, in short repair and restore proper functioning of my nervous system

Ma Kali's favorite planet Saturn represents discipline, boundaries, and the hard-earned wisdom that comes through accepting life's challenges rather than avoiding them. Saturn's lessons are often difficult but ultimately liberating, teaching us that true freedom comes not from having no limitations but from accepting the limitations we cannot change while transforming those we can.

The traditional way to work skillfully with Saturn's energy is through devotion to Goddess Kali.

Kali's skin is depicted as dark blue bordering on black—the color that contains all other colors, representing the formless void from which all emerges and to which it returns. Her long, unkempt black hair flows wild and free, unconfined by social conventions or attempts to make the divine feminine acceptable to patriarchal sensibilities.

Her two eyes are bloodshot from witnessing the suffering of the world without looking away, while her third eye blazes open with the fire of direct spiritual perception. Her mouth gapes wide with a blood-stained tongue protruding—not in a gesture of mockery but as the primal scream of a mother who will destroy anything that threatens her children's awakening.

She stands naked except for a necklace of fifty-two human heads representing the letters of the Sanskrit alphabet—the building blocks of our reality—and a skirt made of human hands. Her nakedness symbolizes absolute truth. The hands that form her skirt represent the creative power that lies dormant within human potential.

Her four arms carry the tools of transformation: her upper left hand holds a freshly severed head (the death of ego-identification), while her lower left holds a skull cup to collect the dripping blood (new life emerging from the compost of what has died). Her upper right hand brandishes a sword (the discriminating wisdom that cuts through illusion), while her lower right carries a trident representing the three fundamental qualities of nature—*sattva* (clarity), *rajas* (activity), and *tamas* (inertia).

Most striking of all, her right foot is placed firmly on the chest of Lord Shiva, pinning him to the ground. This is not a gesture of dominance but of awakening—the consciousness or shiva.

The primordial female energy manifests everything that exists in our universe, while Shiva infuses it with *prana*—the breath of life.

One dark December evening, as fog wrapped around our house like a meditation shawl, I filled the bathtub with warm water scented with rosemary essential oil, lit one of Gwen's handmade soy candles, and took my usual dose of plant medicine.

As I settled into the warm water, feeling my nervous system begin to soften and open, I found myself in that liminal space between waking and dreaming where visions can unfold with startling clarity.

A massive crystal appeared before me. Standing atop this crystal was Krishna, the divine beloved, lost in the music of his flute. The melody seemed to emanate not just from the instrument but from the crystal itself, as if the entire universe were singing.

Then I heard a sound that made my blood freeze—a long, sibilant hiss that spoke of ancient power awakening. Looking up beyond Krishna, I saw a magnificent black cobra with five heads. The serpent's forked tongue flicked out and suddenly I found myself transported through space and time.

I stood before Ma Kali in all her terrible magnificence, blood dripping from her protruding tongue. Rather than fear, I felt an overwhelming sense of coming home—as if I had been searching for this fearsome mother my entire life.

"Ma," I heard myself pleading, "please cut off my head with your sword and add it to the necklace of heads you wear. I am ready to die."

What happened next dissolved all sense of linear time and rational understanding. There was a sound like cosmic suction, and I found myself flying through space directly into Kali's gaping mouth.

Before my mind could process what was happening, I was expelled from her vagina, slick with blood and cosmic fluid. I understood with cellular certainty that I had just been reborn from the goddess's womb—that the woman who had entered this vision was not the same being who was emerging from it.

I threw myself into yoga, pranayama, and meditation with the intensity of someone who has glimpsed the summit and will accept nothing less than reaching it.

The plant medicine and Kali's blessing had opened doors in my awareness, but walking through those doors required consistent, disciplined practice.

My body began to tell me about its stories with unprecedented clarity. My right leg was noticeably longer than my left, creating a cascade of compensations throughout my entire structure. The right side of my pelvis rotated outward, causing my right foot to carry most of my body weight on its outer edge and disrupting the fundamental symmetry that allows the nervous system to function optimally.

This misalignment meant that my right big toe—what yogic anatomy calls "the leader of the foot"—could not exercise its natural intelligence. The difference in leg length had even caused my right foot to grow half a size larger than my left, as if my body were trying to create stability through asymmetrical expansion.

I could feel a knot the size of a golf ball lodged above my right hip, hard and semi-permanent like crystallized tension. A smaller but similar knot had formed on the outside of my left bicep. Both were roadmaps of trauma written in muscle and fascia.

The perpetual imbalance caused by carrying disproportionate weight on my right side kept both feet in a state of chronic stress. They were frequently swollen and sweaty, making shoes slip and slide in ways that terrified my ten toes, each of which seemed to have developed its own anxiety disorder.

My right ear had been compromised for years, with the Eustachian tube chronically clogged and swollen. This affected not just my hearing but my ability to appreciate the subtle differences in tone and pitch that make music and poetry come alive.

Most significantly, I began to understand that my Muladhara chakra—the root center that governs our basic sense of safety and survival—was being constantly challenged by an autonomic nervous system locked in a state of freeze. This is the nervous system response that occurs when fight or flight are not options, when the only way to survive overwhelming circumstances is to shut down and wait for the danger to pass.

The problem was that for me, the danger had passed decades ago, but my nervous system had never received the message that it was safe to fully return to life.

This was etched out in both of my palms: the telltale signs of childhood trauma and nervous system dysregulation.

I began the slow work of correcting these deep patterns of compensation and protection. Every morning, I would spend time simply standing, learning to distribute my weight equally between both feet, feeling my way back to the natural bilateral symmetry that trauma had disrupted.

I practiced walking with consciousness, paying attention to how each step could either reinforce old patterns or create new ones. I learned to place equal pressure on the toes of both feet, awakening neural pathways that had been dormant for years.

Gradually, I became able to sit comfortably in full lotus pose—something that had been impossible when my pelvis was locked in chronic rotation. I could squat on the floor for extended periods, reconnecting with a primal posture that modern life had all but eliminated from my movement vocabulary.

As my pelvis found its natural alignment, the length difference between my legs began to equalize. What I had assumed was a structural problem turned out to be largely functional—the result of muscular holding patterns that could be unwound through patient, conscious attention.

The misalignments had also affected my breathing patterns in ways I had never recognized. I discovered that I had been breathing predominantly through my left nostril for years. According to yogic science, a healthy nervous system naturally alternates nostril dominance throughout each twenty-four-hour period, with both nostrils becoming active during transitional periods called *sandhi*.

This alternating breath pattern reflects the natural rhythm of the autonomic nervous system, balancing sympathetic activation (right nostril/left brain) with parasympathetic relaxation (left nostril/right brain). My chronic left-nostril breathing indicated that I had been stuck in a pattern of withdrawal and internal focus—protective but ultimately limiting.

Breath, I learned, is literally the bridge between voluntary and involuntary nervous system activities. By bringing consciousness to my breathing patterns, I could directly influence my autonomic state in ways that years of talking therapy had never achieved.

I became aware of my habitually shallow and rapid breathing style—the respiratory signature of chronic anxiety—and began consciously extending my exhalations to twice the length of my inhalations. I also experimented with *kumbhaka* (breath retention), holding my breath briefly between inhalations and exhalations to strengthen my capacity to remain calm in the space between action and reaction.

Within two years of beginning this integrated approach to healing—combining plant medicine, spiritual practice, somatic awareness, and conscious movement—symptoms that had plagued me for decades began to dissolve.

I could almost watch the lines transforming on my palms: signs of wisdom and creativity grew, and the heart line lengthened toward the pointer finger, my left thumb got stronger, the three bracelet lines on my wrists became more robust. And lines form the Rahu area on my palms began to travel up to the Jupiter, Saturn, Sun and Mercury points on the palm just below the fingers.

The chronic swelling and excessive sweating in my hands and feet disappeared, as if my nervous system had finally learned to regulate temperature and circulation efficiently. The headaches that had been my companions for years disappeared. The golf ball-sized knot above my right hip and the smaller knot in my left bicep slowly melted, releasing decades of held tension. The feeling of doom at the pit of my stomach disappeared and my elimination routine became like clockwork.

Most significantly, the "black clouds" that had seemed perpetually gathered me—that sense of chronic depression that had colored every experience—began to dissipate like morning fog touched by sunlight.

In place of the familiar landscape of anxiety and despair, seeds of self-love and self-acceptance began to sprout. For the first time in my adult life, I could greet each day with genuine enthusiasm rather than the grim determination that had carried me through previous decades.

Gratitude became my new normal—the natural effervescence of a nervous system that finally felt safe enough to appreciate the beauty and wonder that had always been present around me.

The blind turtle has not only found the ring in the vast ocean but has learned to swim with grace through whatever currents arise. The journey continues, but now it unfolds as play rather than struggle, as devotion rather than seeking, as service rather than survival.

May all beings find their way to the fierce mother's embrace.
May all beings discover the roses hidden within their hearts.
May all beings have the courage to pull the weeds and endure the pain.
May all beings awaken to their true nature.

Om Jayanti Mangala Kali
Bhadrakali Kapalini
Durga Xama Shivadatri
Swaha Swadha Namostute

www.ingramcontent.com/pod-product-compliance
Lightning Source LLC
Chambersburg PA
CBHW020932090426
42736CB00010B/1116